Thirty-Three Ways to Help with Spelling

Thirty-Three Ways to Help with Spelling equips teachers and teaching assistants with a wide range of practical resources to help children who are having difficulties learning the basic skills of spelling.

Offering a range of activities and games to engage children and encourage motivation in the classroom, this essential classroom companion provides ready-to-use material that doesn't need lengthy forward preparation. Activities include auditory and visual mnemonics, phonetics and tactile tasks.

These practical and fun ideas incorporate a variety of learning styles, using kinaesthetic and auditory techniques, that put the emphasis on 'games' rather than 'work'. The activities are especially suitable for teaching assistants working with individuals or small groups. The book works step-by-step through practical activities which:

- keep children motivated and enjoying learning;
- don't require extensive knowledge or experience from the adult;
- are adult-led so children don't have the opportunity to repeat mistakes;
- are grouped into different basic skills, so teachers can choose the activity best suited for the child's needs;
- have clear, concise and pedagogically sound reasons for the activity;
- include extension activities where appropriate to challenge pupils.

This book is aimed mainly at primary pupils, but secondary teachers will also find it invaluable for use with pupils who are falling behind. The series facilitates good inclusive provision and is a resource from which useful ideas and materials can be taken without having to plough through chapters of theory and research.

Heather Morris is a specialist teacher with a learning support service. She has taught in primary schools and in a unit for pupils with specific learning difficulties/dyslexia.

Sue Smith has been a primary school SENCO and Reading Recovery teacher, who now specialises in one-to-one teaching of children with specific learning difficulties/dyslexia.

Thirty-Three Ways to Help with . . .

Supporting children who struggle with basic skills

Series Editor: Linda Evans

This series of practical 'how-to' books is for teachers, teaching assistants and SENCOs who are in need of fresh ideas to teach pupils in their care who are struggling with basic skills. Each title provides tools enabling practitioners to make good provision for a range of children in their class. Practical ideas and materials can be extracted without having to plough through chapters of theory and research.

All titles are A4 in format, photocopiable, and include an introduction and clearly presented activity pages.

Written by experienced practitioners and experts, this series is a lifeline to anyone facing the challenge of teaching children who are struggling.

Other titles in this series:

Thirty-Three Ways to Help with Numeracy by Brian Sharp
Thirty-Three Ways to Help with Reading by Raewyn Hickey
Thirty-Three Ways to Help with Writing by Raewyn Hickey

Thirty-Three Ways to Help with Spelling

Supporting children who struggle with basic skills

Heather Morris and Sue Smith

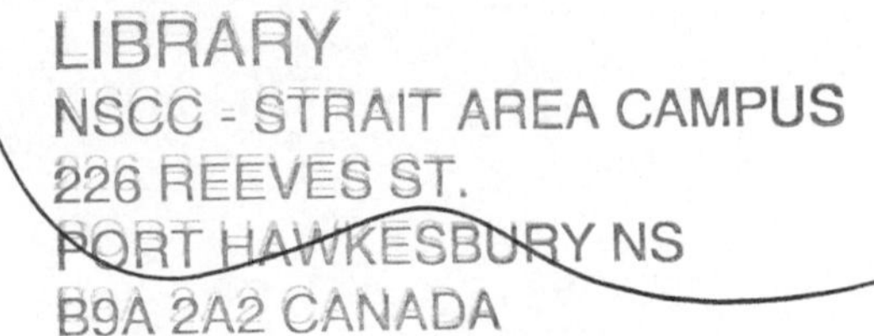

First edition published 2011
by Routledge
2 Park Square, Milton Park, Abingdon, Oxon, OX14 4RN

Simultaneously published in the USA and Canada
by Routledge
270 Madison Avenue, New York, NY 10016

Routledge is an imprint of the Taylor & Francis Group, an informa business

Typeset in Bembo and Futura by
Keystroke, Tettenhall, Wolverhampton
Printed and bound in Great Britain by
MPG Books Group, UK

British Library Cataloguing in Publication Data
A catalogue record for this book is available from the British Library

Library of Congress Cataloging-in-Publication Data
Morris, Heather, teacher.
Thirty-Three Ways to help with spelling: supporting children who struggle with basic skills / Heather Morris and Sue Smith. – 1st ed.
p. cm.
1. English language – Orthography and spelling – Study and teaching (Elementary) – Activity programs. I. Smith, Sue, teacher. II. Title. III. Title: Thirty-three ways to help with spelling.
LB1574.M59 2010
372.63′2044 – dc22 2009053864

ISBN10: 0–415–56080–2 (pbk)
ISBN10: 0–203–84830–6 (ebk)

ISBN13: 978–0–415–56080–1 (pbk)
ISBN13: 978–0–203–84830–2 (ebk)

Contents

Thirty-three ways to help . . . the series

This is a series of books to help teachers, teaching assistants and parents who want to help children to learn.

Most children at some stage or other in their school life come across something that they find difficult; a small minority of learners have difficulty in grasping the basic ideas presented in many lessons. Whichever the case, there is a need for extra explanation and practice so that children can unravel any misconceptions, understand what is being taught and move on. Very often nowadays, this extra practice – or 'reinforcement' – is provided by teaching assistants (TAs) who are such a valuable resource in our schools.

Planning activities for TAs to use with children who need extra help can be challenging, however. There is little time to design 'mini-lessons' for TAs to use with individuals or small groups of children – and to talk them through the 'delivery' of such activities. This is exactly where the **Thirty-Three Ways** series comes into play.

Teachers will be able to choose an appropriate activity for individuals or groups as part of their structured programme, or as a 'one-off' lesson for extra practice. The games and activities require no prior theoretical reading or knowledge and little or no preparation, and can be easily used by TAs or volunteer helpers in the classroom; teachers may also wish to share some activities with parents who want to know how to support their children at home. The activities use a multi-sensory approach to learning – visual, auditory and kinaesthetic; they have been designed for children aged 6–11 years, who need additional help with particular skills and concepts.

Teachers are constantly challenged to find ways to keep pupils motivated and to give them worthwhile 'catch-up' opportunities. But much of the photocopiable material available to teachers is too often 'busy work' which keeps children 'occupied' as opposed to learning. The books in this series provide a variety of adult-led activities that will keep children interested and take them forward in their learning. In this way, their confidence and self-esteem will grow as they experience success and have fun at the same time.

Series features

- Activities are enjoyable and multi-sensory, to keep children motivated and enjoying learning.
- Activities do not require a lot of preparation and any materials required are provided or readily available in classrooms.
- Activities are adult-led so children do not have the opportunity to keep repeating the same mistakes.
- Activities are grouped into different basic skill areas, so teachers can choose the activity best suited for the child's needs.
- Clear, concise reasons are set out for each activity.
- Extension activity is given where appropriate, to challenge pupils and extend their learning.

Acknowledgements

We would like to thank staff and pupils at The Ridge Primary School, Stourbridge for their help with trialling some of the activities included in this book.

The Learning Support Service in Dudley must also be acknowledged as it is through working for the Service that we have developed our knowledge and skills over the years

We would also like to thank Dr Colin Smith for his essential technological support and encouragement.

Introduction

Some children learn to spell without any difficulty at all. They are the lucky ones. However you will encounter many who have difficulty in learning to spell words, especially the 'tricky' ones. This book is designed to help you to help the children you are involved with, to become better spellers and to ensure that they learn with enjoyment.

Many children who have spelling difficulties will have low self-esteem and may try to avoid writing whenever they can. This can often lead to avoidance tactics and behavioural difficulties. Teaching should not be about learning long lists of words in an uninteresting way. The games and activities in this book are aimed at making learning to spell an interesting and fun process.

There are many reasons for spelling difficulties:

- Spelling is above all a memory activity, and many children have visual and auditory memory difficulties.
- Teachers' expectations can be too high. As teachers, we need to start at a level at which every child can succeed.
- Many children have not been taught explicitly *how* to learn spellings.
- Teaching approaches may not have matched different learning styles. Children can be visual, auditory, tactile or kinaesthetic learners. They need to acquire strategies for learning words that match their learning styles.
- New spellings are not always sufficiently practised to consolidate learning.

Some children will learn to spell words but will have difficulty with long-term retention. They will learn to spell words and get them right on the day of the test but will have forgotten them a week later, or continue to spell them incorrectly in their written work, often in several different ways in one piece of writing. This is because they have not learned the words to a sufficient depth for the words to have transferred into long-term memory. They will not have achieved automaticity. If the pupil has to pause and think before writing a word it has not been learned adequately. A good way of explaining this to a child is to say, 'It should drop off the end of your pen'. They need to understand that practice makes perfect.

The purpose of this book is to help you help the weak spellers to overcome their difficulties in a fun way.

This book is divided into three sections:

- A. Spelling Strategies
- B. Phonic Activities
- C. Games for Spelling Practice.

We suggest that the first section – 'Spelling strategies' – is made a priority. Many children who are weak spellers have not acquired strategies to help them to learn to spell different kinds of words.

The other two sections can be dipped into without following any particular order.

The games and activities have been planned so that they can be made quickly, using materials available in school together with the photocopiable material in the book.

Don't forget: have fun!

Before you begin, remember to follow the golden rules.

The golden rules

By following a few simple rules, you will be able to take full advantage of the suggestions in the rest of the book and maximise the effectiveness of the approaches described.

- Ask children to learn only one list of words. Too often we encounter those who are learning one set of words for the teacher, another list for the teaching assistant, and so on.
- Link the number of words to the child's learning capabilities. Some will only manage one or two words each week. It is better to learn two words thoroughly than ten words which will be forgotten next week.
- Limit the maximum number of words to no more than five for children with spelling difficulties. The 'Learn a Word a Day' routine is useful, with revision at the weekend.
- Choose words that are going to be most useful to the child in everyday writing, and which are within their capability to learn.
- Demonstrate to all children that different learning strategies can be used for different types of words. The first section of this book introduces a range of strategies.
- Remember that children will have different learning styles – visual, auditory and kinaesthetic.
- Discuss different learning strategies with parents and carers. A spelling workshop for parents is useful.
- Encourage the five minutes a day routine. Parents need to be aware that the 'little and often' approach is best.

- Supply each word in a simple sentence whenever possible. When testing, ask the children to write the sentence but only mark the target words. This will help them to transfer words to independent writing.
- Link spelling and handwriting together. The children should be encouraged to use a cursive script. There is a proven link between a good flow of joined handwriting and accurate spelling.
- Be positive. Many children with spelling problems have low self-esteem. Don't forget words are never wrong but 'nearly right'.
- Mark positively. Try ticking the words that have been spelled correctly and throw away the red pen. Tick individual letters and highlight the incorrect ones.

Remember

Any spelling activity should be fun.

Praise!

Always vary your words of praise. The alphabetical list opposite makes some suggestions but try to add more of your own, selecting and using those which come most naturally to you and will be most meaningful to the child.

Praise words: an alphabetical list

amazing	ace	awesome
beautiful	best	brilliant
champion	clever	cool
dazzling	delightful	dreamy
easy peasy	excellent	exceptional
fabulous	fantastic	first class
grand	great	good
heavenly	hooray	hunky-dory
improving	incredible	interesting
jolly good	joyful	just right
keen	knockout	knowledgeable
like it	lovely	luscious
magnificent	marvellous	much improved
neat	near perfection	nice
on target	out of this world	outstanding
perfect	personal best	pretty fine
quality	quick	quantity
really great	remarkable	round of applause
sensational	splendid	super
terrific	tip top	tremendous
unbelieveable	unstoppable	unsurpassed
valuable effort	vastly improved	victorious
wicked	wonderful	wow
x factor – talent	yippee!	zero mistakes

A. Spelling strategies

A good speller can look at a word, decide how to remember the various parts and once they have learned it, they can revisualise it and spell it correctly.

A poor speller will look at a word and probably try to remember it by looking at each individual letter. This is a time-consuming and inefficient way of learning to spell. Weak spellers have not acquired strategies to help them become good spellers. They need to be shown a range of strategies and encouraged to find which works best for them.

The activities in this section of the book demonstrate and provide practice in using a range of strategies which will help individuals find the best way for them to learn spellings more effectively.

A poor speller tends to rely on one or two senses, usually visual and/or auditory, often not even using these approaches efficiently. The activities in this section encourage more effective use of visual and auditory approaches and also show poor spellers how to use multi-sensory strategies, including tactile and kinaesthetic senses.

- *Visual* approaches involve looking at the *shape* of letters and words.
- *Auditory* approaches involve hearing and saying the *sound* of phonemes and words.
- *Tactile* approaches involve *touching* and *feeling* letters.
- *Kinaesthetic* approaches involve awareness of movement in *writing* words.

These activities also emphasise the importance of being able to see the word in the mind's eye, in other words, to visualise it before trying to write it.

ACTIVITY 1

Teaching the tricks: how to learn to spell words

This is to show children how to learn to spell different kinds of words and to develop an interest in words.

Children need to be taught to look carefully at words. They need to know that different kinds of words can be learned in different ways. Discuss each word and try to think of as many different ways of learning to spell it.

These are some ways to 'trick' the memory and help children to learn words so that they will never forget them.

Resources

- Paper
- Soft-lead pencils or felt-tip pens.
- Whiteboard/pen.

Preparation

- Adult selects target words.

Activity

- Adult says each word as it sounds, and child repeats it.

Wed – nes – day, Feb – ru – ary, no – thing

- Adult taps out syllables and child joins in.

yes – ter – day, re – mem – ber, hos – pit – al

- Adult prompts child to look for words within words.

t(hat), fat/her

- Adult prompts child to look at the shape of the word. Adult asks child, *How many letters are above/below the line?*

- Adult and child chant or sing out loud.

h-a-p-p-y

O-U-T says out

- Look for patterns in words.

M*ar*tin, Sm*ar*ties, M*ar*s B*ar*

- Adult introduces a rule if appropriate. Look at the most common ones, e.g. 'i' before 'e' (but acknowledge that there are some exceptions).

- Try a silly sentence.

The knight in knitted knickers.

- Highlight the tricky part of the word.

c al m

- Is there another way?

'i to end will be a friend' or 'You can "fri" end'

- Children are very inventive – they may be able to think of other ways.

ACTIVITY 2

Feely bag

This is a way to use tactile cues to help children learn new spellings and reinforce their spelling of known words.

Some children who need help with auditory and visual sequencing benefit from using a tactile cue to focus on the shape and orientation of letters. They need to think more purposefully about the construction of the whole word, not just its beginning or general shape. Be aware that this activity may not be suitable if the child is confusing *b/d/p*. However, some older children may enjoy the challenge of trying to find the correct orientation of such 'difficult' letters.

Resources

- Three-dimensional magnetic letters (lower case).
- Magnetic whiteboard.
- Small bag which child cannot see through.
- Phoneme frame, or draw phoneme frame on whiteboard.

Preparation

- Select words from child's list of target spellings.
- If child is having difficulties with letter orientation, e.g. *b/d/p* or *u/n*, choose words without problem letters.

Activity

- Adult makes target word on magnetic board, child reads word.
- Child places letters in feely bag in correct sequence.
- Child shakes letters in the bag.
- Child picks letters out of bag (in correct sequence) and places them correctly in the phoneme frame.

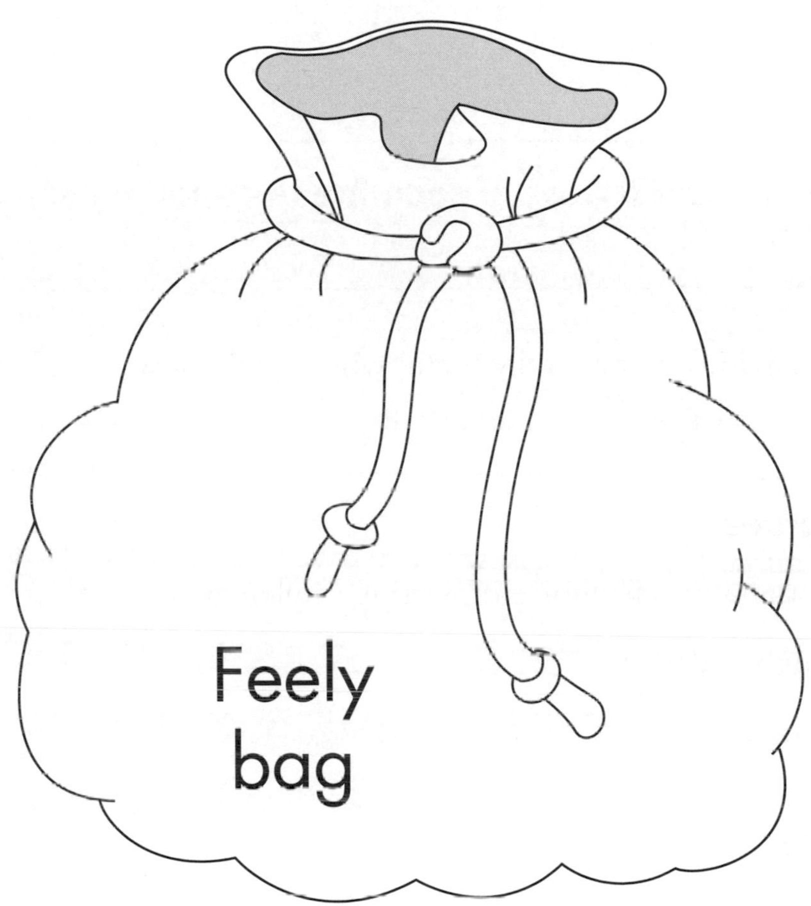

Extension: jumblies

- Adult writes list of three to five target spellings on whiteboard.
- Adult selects one word from list and makes it into a *jumblie* with magnetic letters in wrong order.
- Child compares *jumblie* with target list and rearranges letters to spell word correctly.
- Repeat with other target words.

ACTIVITY 3

Chaining and tracking

These are useful ways of securing the spelling of a target word.

These activities are especially useful when working with an individual but can be adapted for a small group.

Resources

- Paper and pencil/choice of writing implements.
- Whiteboard/pen.
- Plastic letters.

Activity

- Make the target word in plastic letters.

  school

- The child removes first letter then replaces it.
- The child removes the first two letters then replaces them in the correct order.
- Continue until all letters are removed and replaced in the correct order.
- Adult writes the word with the first letter omitted: **-chool**. The child has to fill in the missing letter.

- Continue as above removing letters until the whole word can be written independently.

  - chool - - hool - - - ool - - - - ol - - - - - l - - - - - -

- This process may take several sessions before the word is fixed.
- Assess transfer by checking that the child can spell the word in a simple dictated sentence.
- If unsuccessful return to start.

This method is referred to as forward chaining. Some children may prefer to reverse the process by removing letters from the end of the word – **schoo-, scho--** and so on.

- Once the target word has been learned omit letters at random.

  s-hoo- sc--ol s-ho-l s--oo-

- Try using a speed sheet where the pupil has to fill in the missing letters
- Repeat regularly until the word is secure.

sc-ool	sch--l	s--oo-	---o-l	s-h-ol
s--o-l	sch---	s-h-ol	s--ool	s----l
sc---l	sc-o-l	s-hool	s----l	------

Tracking

Write the target words onto a sheet of paper and ask the group/individual to highlight each letter in order. Then record the word onto the sheet.

school p s t c w z h m o v o q a e l -------------

The chaining and tracking activities can be extended by asking them to write each known word in a simple sentence.

ACTIVITY 4

Getting a feeling for words

Different senses are important in learning to spell. Using multisensory approaches ensures that children are not limited to using only one of their sensory channels.

In addition to visual and auditory activities some children find that tactile and kinaesthetic approaches work best. This literally gives them a feeling for words.

Here are a number of ways in which you can encourage children to gain a different 'feel' for words by tracing and writing them using different media.

Resources

These will depend on the activities chosen – details are provided below.

Activities

The child:

- writes a word in sand, or on textured wallpaper, felt, shaving foam;
- traces over sandpaper letters with their fingers;
- uses a thick brush to paint letters/words on large piece of paper;

- uses a large decorator's brush dipped in water to paint words on slabs, path, etc.;
- uses a water pistol or squeezy bottle filled with water to write words on outside wall, path, etc.;
- writes on condensation on steamy window;
- uses variety of writing implements, e.g. thick and thin pencils, pens, glitter/gel pens, highlighters;
- writes inside lines of hollow letters

- makes words with playdoh, Wicki Stix, Fuzzy Felt, pipecleaners;
- writes word in the air, on pupil/teacher's back;
- cuts out large-print letters from newspapers or magazines and makes words by sticking them onto paper;
- shines torch onto dark paper to spell word.

ACTIVITY 5

SOS: simultaneous oral spelling

This is a way of teaching pupils to spell short irregular 'tricky' words.

Simultaneous oral spelling is a multi-sensory spelling method that utilises all the senses. The pupil must know all the letter names to be able to apply this method.

It is useful for working one-to-one with a child. It can be demonstrated to parents for use at home.

Resources

- Paper/whiteboard.
- Pens/pencils.

Activity

- The adult writes the word (preferably in a cursive script) and says it out loud.
- The child:
  - repeats the word;
  - traces over the word several times saying the letter names;
  - copies the word saying the letter names as s/he writes;

  - then writes the word from memory;
  - then checks the attempt.
- Adult praises correct spelling.
- Remember if incorrect the word is not wrong but 'nearly right'.
- If incorrect, the adult highlights the 'tricky' part of the word with a highlighter pen and then starts the process again.

Practising SOS: spelling boxes

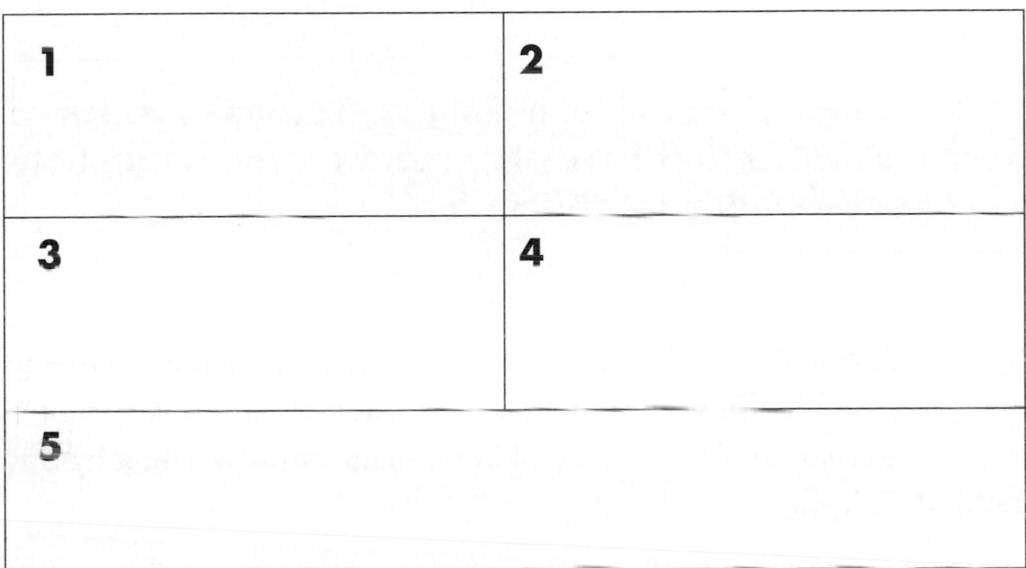

Box 1: Teacher writes the word in bold script and reads it.

The child repeats the word and then writes over it six times using different coloured pens and saying letter names.

Box 2: The child copies the word as many times as possible.

Box 3: Fold the paper to cover boxes 1 and 2. The child then writes from memory. If the word is spelled correctly the child proceeds to box 4 (after plenty of praise). If the word is incorrect highlight the tricky part of the word and start again at box 1. Don't forget that misspelt words are 'nearly right'.

Box 4: The word is written several times with eyes closed.

Box 5: The word is written in a simple sentence. Mark only the target word but praise other words correctly spelled.

ACTIVITY 6

Make a mnemonic

This approach is useful for helping to fix those very tricky words or words that have persistent errors. It can help to correct sequencing difficulties.

Mnemonics are memory prompts, or 'tricks' to help children remember spellings and other facts. These can be auditory or visual prompts and are often lots of fun so that children usually enjoy learning by this method.

Children are more likely to retain words if they are encouraged to think of their own mnemonic, the sillier the better. There are some familiar mnemonics that have been 'tried and tested'. You will need to use them regularly to help children remember them at first.

This activity is useful for working with individuals and small groups.

Resources

- Paper/whiteboard.
- Pens/pencils.

Examples of auditory mnemonics

because = **b**ake **e**leven **c**akes **a**nd **u**se **s**ix **e**ggs

or

big **e**lephants **c**ry **a**nd **u**pset **s**mall **e**lephants

or

big **e**lephants **c**an **a**dd **u**p **s**ums **e**asily

could/would/should = o u lazy **d**ogs

night/light/sight etc = I go **h**ome **t**onight

enough/cough = only **u**gly **g**iants **h**itchhike

Tuesday = u eat **s**weets day

people = people **e**at **o**ranges **p**eople **l**ike **e**ggs

beautiful = big **e**lephants **a**re **u**gly . . . ti . . . ful

Examples of visual mnemonics

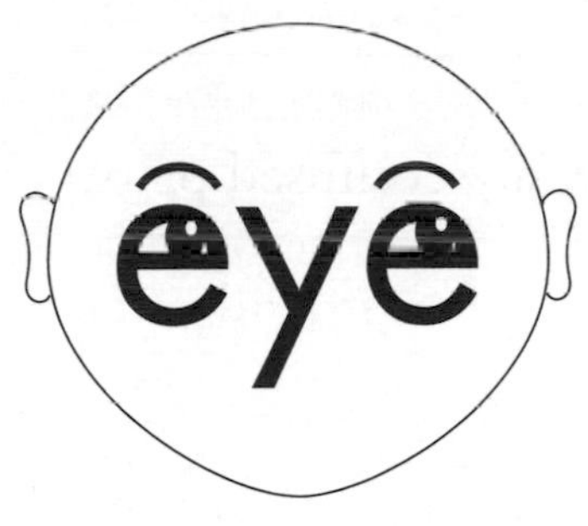

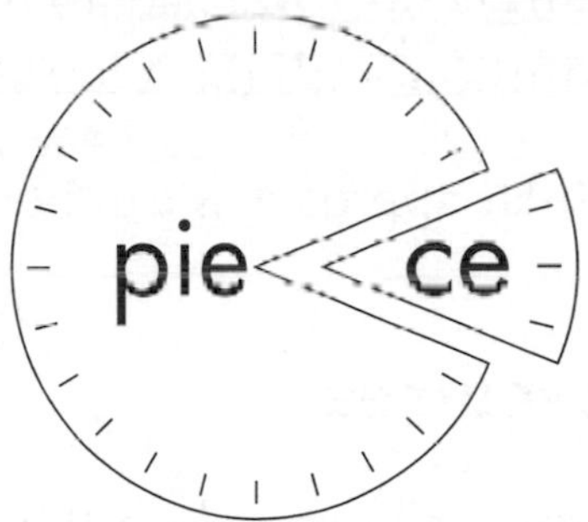

Activity

Select a word that the group or individual persistently misspells and see if they can make a mnemonic to help them learn it: 'said' and 'they' immediately come to mind!

ACTIVITY 7

Letter confusions

This is a way to reduce confusion between visually similar letters.

Poor spellers often reverse certain letters, for example *b/d*; *p/q*; *m/n*; *f/t*.

Concentrating on one letter until it is established helps reduce confusion. Is the letter in the child's name? Can it be related to a familiar word, e.g. a favourite pet, pop star, or a TV programme?

Examples below relate to reinforcing the shape of the letter *b* to prevent confusion with the letter *d*.

Similar approaches can be used with other easily confused pairs.

Resources

These will depend on the activity chosen.

Activity

- Highlight *b* on photocopied sheet of mixed letters.
- Highlight *b* in words on pages (enlarged) from newspapers, magazines, and comics.
- Trace a large *b* on whiteboard, wall or playground, with torch or water pistol, using big arm movement.

- Make *b* with plasticene, playdoh, pipecleaners, Wikki Stix.
- Feeling *b* in different textures – sandpaper, felt, textured wallpaper, sand.
- Rol 'n' Write: marble rolls the correct way around grooved letter *b*.
- Letter boxes:

1 b	2
3	4

1. Adult models, child writes over with rainbow colours.
2. Child copies.
3. Child writes from memory.
4. Child writes with eyes closed.

Prompts

Encourage the child to try different prompts until they find one which they are happy to use as a reminder when working. Examples below refer specifically to *b/d*:

- Child makes shapes of *b/d* with fingers.

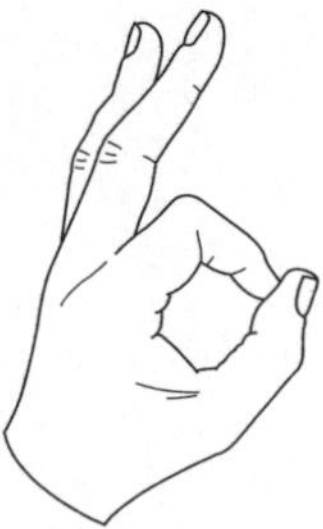

- Child makes fists with thumbs extended.

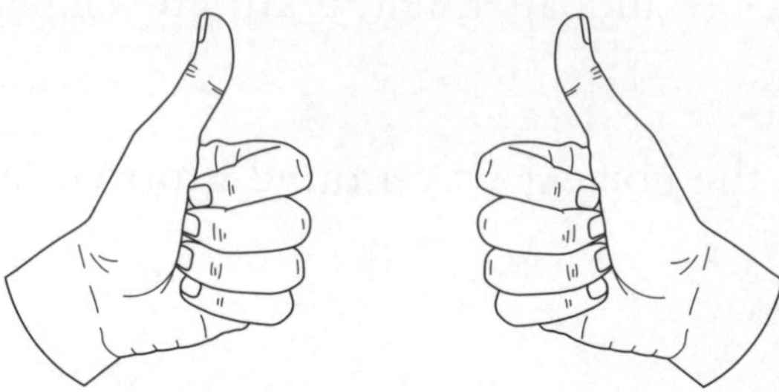

- Adult draws picture of a bed. Child highlights *b*/*d*.

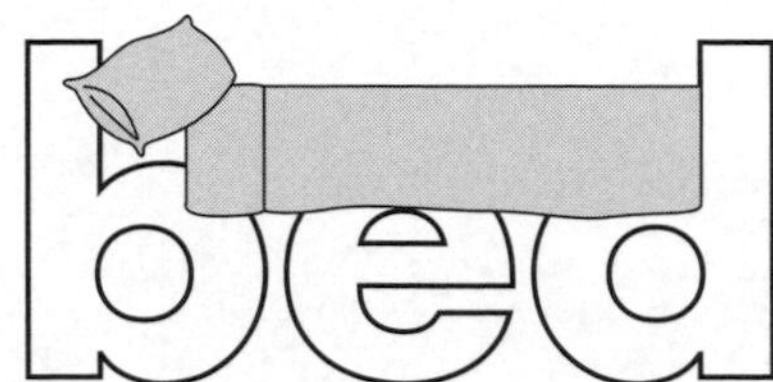

- Adult draws bat and ball to show how *b* is formed.

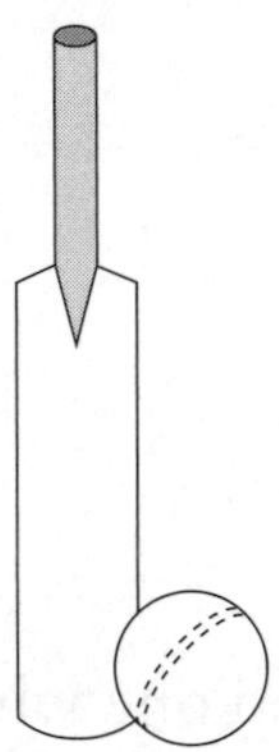

- Child highlights *b* (lower case) as the bottom half of capital *B*.

- Written prompts:

  Child writes *a b c d* at top of each page.

  Child writes *b* on top left and *d* on top right of each page.

ACTIVITY 8

Look, say, cover, write, check

This is a way to practise revisualisation of words.

Good spellers are able to 'revisualise', which means to picture the word in their mind. Poor spellers find it difficult to picture the whole word and try to copy spellings letter by letter. This activity gives children practice in learning strategies to help them revisualise the whole word.

Resources

- Strips of card.
- Whiteboard and pen.
- Paper and pencil.
- Plastic/magnetic letters.

Preparation

- Write each target spelling on a separate strip of card.

Activity

Ask the child to:

Look

- Look carefully at the letters in the word.
- Look at the shape.
- Look at the letters that go above and below the line.
- Try to visualise the pattern.
- Look for tricky parts.

Say

- Trace the word with finger and say it out loud using letter names.
- Trace it in the air, on the table, on someone's back.
- Close your eyes and see it on your eyelids.
- Imagine it on the computer screen.

Cover

- Child covers with hand, paper or writing flap or turns word over.
- Child closes eyes again to revisualise the word.

Write

- Child writes the word from memory saying the letter names.

Check

- Child looks at word carefully and checks spelling by ticking each correct letter.
- If incorrect, child highlights the incorrect letters and discusses which were the 'tricky' parts.
- Child tries again by repeating the process from 'Look'.
- If still incorrect, try using plastic or magnetic letters.
- If correct, ask child to try writing the word with their eyes closed.

said
fold under

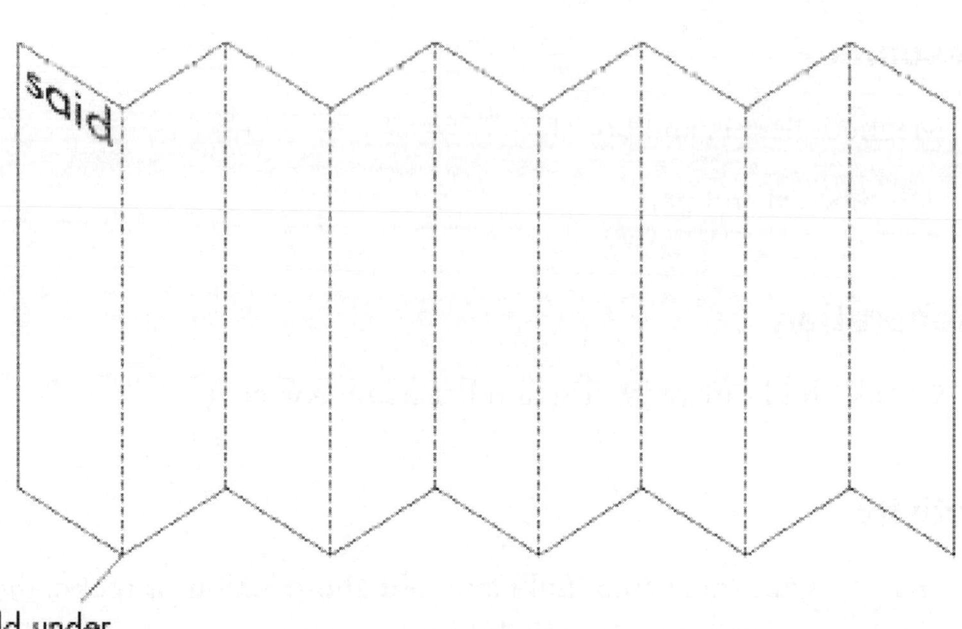

ACTIVITY 9

Essential spellings

Children must learn to write their full names. They should also be able to write their address and date of birth. In addition it is useful for the child to be able to correctly spell the names of other family members and pets.

Resources

- Magnetic letters and board.
- Whiteboard and pen.

Preparation

- Check child can write first and last name correctly.

Activity

- Starting with first name (full name not abbreviation or nickname), emphasise starting with capital letter.
- Practise making name with magnetic letters.
- Child then writes name on whiteboard.
- Repeat with last name.
- Practise daily until child writes both names accurately and confidently.

- Repeat with address (one line at a time). This may take some time.
- For date of birth and year combine with Calendar cues (Activity 10) to help learn spelling of birthday month.
- Continue with brothers, sisters and family pets.
- Then practise question words: *who, what, when, where, why*. Direct the child's attention to the common start of question words: *wh*.

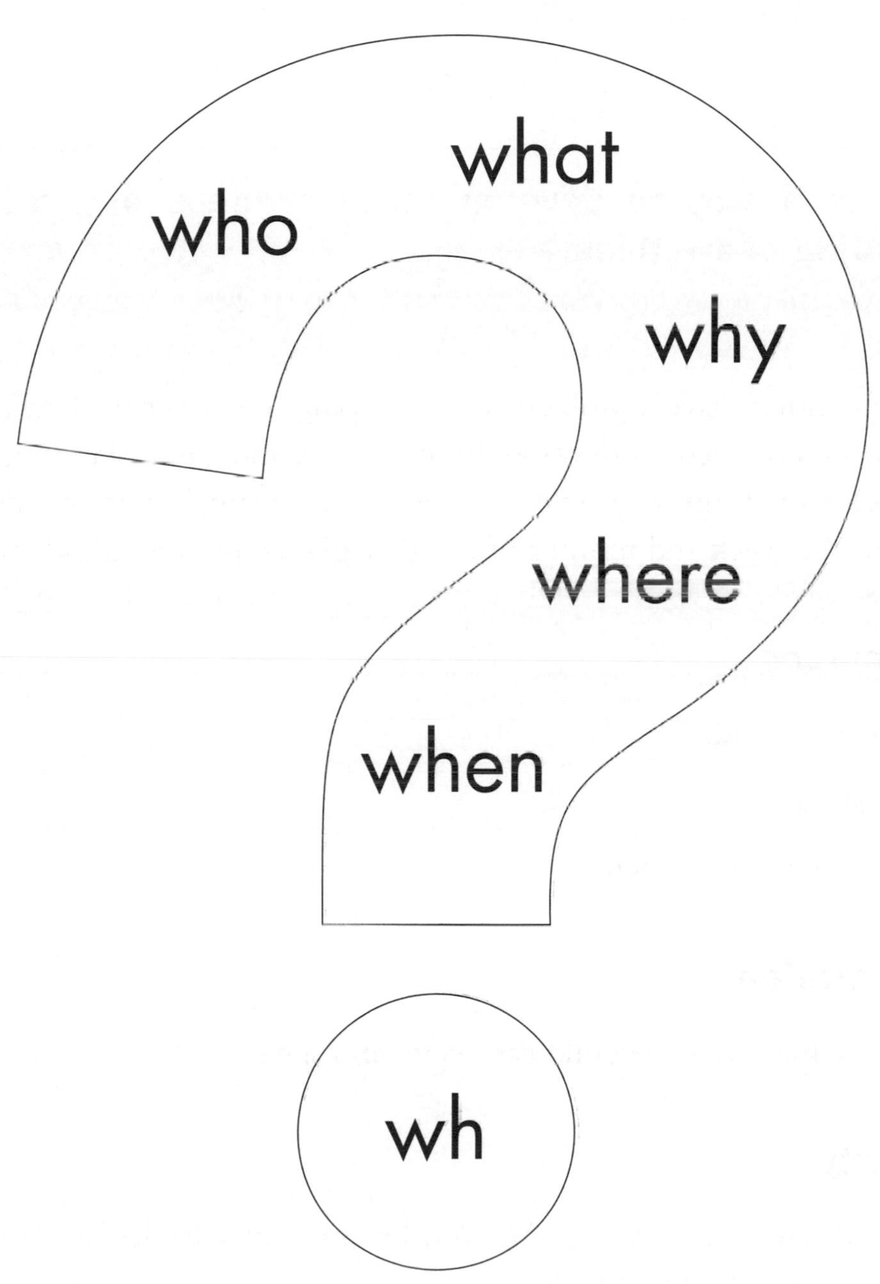

ACTIVITY 10

Calendar cues

This is a way to develop an awareness and understanding of syllables.

Some children have a problem with grasping the concept of syllabification. They need to develop an awareness and understanding that words are made up of syllables. Choosing useful and familiar words like days of the week and months of the year gives children confidence.

Resources

- Strips of card.
- Scissors.
- Whiteboard and pen.

Preparation

Check which days the child can recite and spell.

Activity

- Adult says cue word e.g. *Monday*, beating out syllables by clapping hands or tapping on table.

  Mon – day

- Child practises repeating word whilst clapping/tapping out syllables.

- Adult writes word on long strip of card.
- Adult and child repeat word tapping out syllables and agree where to mark syllable break with dotted line.
- Word is then cut into syllables.
- Ask the child to look for the vowel in each syllable.
- Child rearranges and sounds out cut syllables as word is re-assembled.
- Adult covers word and child repeats word emphasising syllables.
- Child attempts to revisualise and write word.
- If the child finds writing the whole word too difficult, ask the child to write one cut-up syllable at a time until they are able to remember the whole word.
- Split *Tues – day* into two syllables – explain one syllable can contain more than one vowel.
- *Wed – nes – day*, pronouncing *d* in first syllable until child knows spelling.
- Link *Thursday* with *Saturday* as both have *ur* pattern.

Extension

- Use same method with months.
- Start with child's birthday month.
- Next use current month.

Jan – u – ary, Feb – ru – ary, March, A – pril, May, June, Ju – ly, Au – gust, Sep – tem – ber, Oc – to – ber, No – vem – ber, De – cem – ber

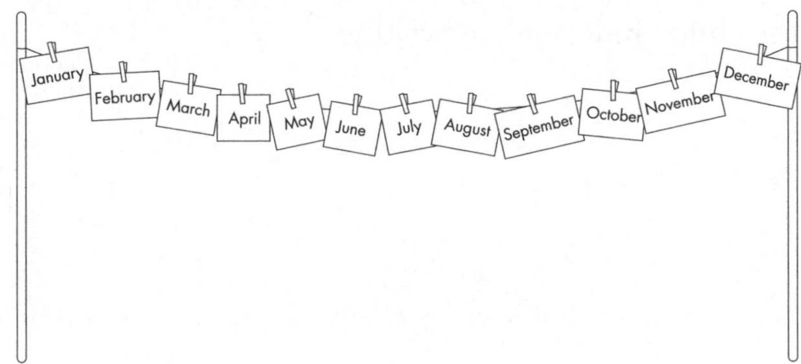

ACTIVITY 11

Freeing speller's block

This is a way to encourage children to gain confidence in free writing.

Poor spellers are reluctant writers. When asked to write a passage as part of class work, they will produce a minimum amount. Often their handwriting is hard to read, with poor letter formation. They do not want or like to see a piece of their work which they know has lots of mistakes and is not easy for anyone to read.

To free poor spellers from this particular form of 'writer's (or speller's) block', the following strategy is very effective in encouraging them to produce writing in quantity and giving them confidence.

The child will see an easy-to-read, presentable version of their work and then with adult help can identify a few errors as targets for improvement.

Resources

A passage of the child's independent writing.

Activity

First session

- The child brings a passage of free writing from work done in class.
- The adult and child read the passage together as soon as possible after it has been written (while the child still remembers it and what they were trying to say).

Between sessions

- Adult types the piece of writing, including spelling errors, and prints it. The adult does this, not the child, because this is about spelling not keyboard skills.
- Adult highlights all correct spellings so child can see how much of the work is already correct.
- Adult analyses errors and sorts into:
  - words almost correct;
  - words which have been learnt but not retained;
  - high frequency words (remember that some words will be low priority, e.g. proper nouns).
- This will help identify a few errors as next teaching targets. It is best to start with words which are almost correct to make success more likely.

Following session

- Adult and child read passage and discuss which two or three spellings they will work on next.
- Child practises these spellings during the week and is encouraged to use these words in the next piece of free writing.
- Date and keep copies of each printed version to show the child his improvement over time.

ACTIVITY 12

Write well, spell well

It is very important to teach handwriting and learning to spell together because this links visual imagery with the kinaesthetic sense of movement.

Spelling well and writing well are closely linked. As children learn joined-up handwriting they gain confidence and are able to write faster. For poor spellers the movement involved in joining letters in a cursive script provides kinaesthetic reinforcement, which they don't receive when printing one letter at a time.

Writing whole words also helps children with getting letters in the right order, left to right orientation, and the regularity of certain letter patterns.

Initially, writing a cursive script will slow the child down but assure them that with practice they will get faster.

Linking handwriting and spelling

Essential points to consider when linking handwriting and spelling involve how letters are formed, how the pen or pencil is gripped, the most appropriate type of lined paper, how joins are taught and practised and giving particular attention to the needs of left-handers.

Resources

- Different types of pens, pencils, crayons.
- Pencil grips.
- Tramlined paper.
- Magnetic letters.

Activity

Letter formation

- Teach correct letter formation, paying attention to:
  - starting points;
  - correct direction and height;
  - exit points.
- Doodling patterns is good practice for making letters the same size. Make patterns using the six strokes needed to form letters.

  /// \\\ --- III ccc ɔɔɔ

  Try to start or finish a spelling session with a bit of pattern doodling.
- Provide lots of different types of pens and pencils. Rollerball pens are ideal as the child does not need to use much pressure. Biros are not usually suitable because they require too much pressure.
- Try to avoid using loops as this is difficult and can be confusing for poor spellers. The simpler the cursive style the better.

Grip

- Check child is using the correct tripod grip, employing forefinger, middle finger and thumb.
- Make sure their grip is not too tense. If they hold the pencil too tightly this is likely to make their arm and shoulder ache.

Lines

- Use tramlined paper with three parallel lines: a top, a mid and a base line. Use a range of line widths: wider or narrower according to size of handwriting.
- Magnetic letters are useful to show the child where letters sit on the line. Sort into tall letters, letters with tails, and so on.

Joining

- If the child is still printing letters, work on words they can already spell and use these for practising joined-up writing.
- Teach short high frequency words first, e.g. *the*, *and*, *is*, *to*, *in*, *was*, *he*, *me*.
- Teach groups of letters as a joined spelling pattern, e.g. *and*, *ent*, *all*, *ump*.

Practise

- Practise a new word by getting the child to write it in a sentence. Only mark for the target word in the sentence.
- Ask the child to write the word with eyes shut so they cannot use visual cues. Once they are happy with writing single words this way, try writing short dictated sentences with eyes closed.

Corrections

If the child does write an incorrect spelling, ask them to try again. Do not let them try to alter the incorrect word by writing over the top of it.

Left-handers

Be aware left-handers need to position paper in an opposite direction to a right-hander, so that they can see what they have written. If children share a table, make sure that left-handers sit to the left of right-handers, so that there is enough room to support their forearms.

B. Phonic activities

From Reception class onwards children will have been taught letter sounds. With poor spellers it is important to check which of these sounds the child knows and which they do not know.

It is important to be positive. Find a starting point where the child is experiencing success and so will approach new tasks with confidence. It is not helpful to focus on failure and what the child doesn't know. Always look for what they *do* know, not what they don't.

Check that the child:

- can hear initial/medial/final sounds;
- can give sounds and names to letters;
- can write a given letter sound or name;
- can match lower case to upper case letters;
- can identify a word from hearing a sequence of sounds;
- can differentiate between vowels and consonants and identify which is which in a word.

When working on the activities in this section encourage the child to stretch the letter sounds as this will help them blend sounds together to make a word. When doing these activities the adult should articulate the word slowly but naturally and ask the child to copy this slow way of saying the word.

ACTIVITY 13

Phoneme fixing

The following suggestions will help children to acquire letter patterns and to sort out spelling choices.

Many children find great difficulty in retaining new phonemes. The activities listed will help them to 'fix the phoneme'. Some children will need to learn by following as many different ways as possible. For others a few will suffice. Several sessions may be needed for a range of activities to be completed.

Resources

- Paper or whiteboards.
- Selection of pens and pencils.
- Copies of text passages.
- Tracing paper/transparency sheets.

Activity

The activities are suitable for individual or small group work. They can be used with other activities and games in this book.

Ideas to try when introducing a new phoneme

- Try to start with a known word

  ai – r*ai*n, *ay* – d*ay*.

- Teach multi-sensory strategies by linking to handwriting (see Activity 12, 'Write well, spell well') – let the child practise writing the phoneme several times using correct letter formation saying the phoneme at the same time.

- Try tracking activities. Circle or highlight the phoneme in a string of letters.

  aiatamanbyaityuaibaighaifatlairrai

- Highlight words containing the phoneme on a sheet of text.

- Let children look through books to find and highlight target words containing the phoneme. (Use tracing paper or a transparency sheet.)

- Make new words on paper, on white boards, phoneme frames (see Activity 15), using plastic letters/Scrabble tiles.

- Establish a clue word for each phoneme. Write it on a card or in a small notebook. Select between five and ten common words that contain the phoneme for learning to spell securely.

- Let the pupil learn to write a silly sentence, e.g. I went to Sp*ai*n and left my sn*ai*l on the tr*ai*n.

- Try 'Minute a Day' type activities, e.g. How many words can they write from dictation in a minute? See Activity 30, 'Speed spelling'.

- Over-learn one phoneme before introducing the next.

- Start each session by a brief recap of the phonemes taught in previous lessons, i.e. reading and spelling 'clue words'.

N.B. There are a number of software packages available to supplement these types of activity and add variety, e.g. Wordshark (www.wordshark.co.uk), Spell Track, Word Track, Phoneme Track (www.semerc.com/product/word-track), or Nessy (www.dyslexic.com/nessy).

Published materials can also be used, e.g. a variety of board games from companies such as Smartkids (www.smartkids.co.uk) and LDA (www.ldalearning.com).

ACTIVITY 14

Clue words and silly sentences

This activity will help to secure the long-term retention of a target phoneme.

It is suitable for working with an individual or small group.

Children with spelling difficulties often have difficulty learning long lists of phonemes. Moreover they find it hard when spelling choices become involved. By learning a clue word (preferably a known one that can be easily illustrated) and between five and ten common words for each phoneme, the learning load is lightened.

Resources

- Notebook or word cards (same size as playing cards).
- Paper/whiteboard.
- Pens and pencils.

Activity

Record any phonemes that the child is finding tricky to spell, in a special notebook or on small individual cards to make a spelling card pack. As more phonemes are introduced, group the phonemes according to spelling choices.

ow (cow), ow (snow), oe (toe), etc.

COW 	how now down town brown
How now brown cow!	

Those with a special interest or hobby such as football, fishing, fashion etc. may like to select a related clue word.

- *Football*: goal, play, score, turf, throw, shirt, foul, game, line, home, rule, feet, bar, etc.
- *Fashion*: hairspray, skirt, new, purse, shorts, powder, coat, heels, glitter, groovy, sleepover, etc.
- *Fishing*: line, hook, perch, roach, pool, stream, float, bait, pike, eel, snail, beetle, trout, etc.
- *Nature*: bird, stoat, hare, eagle, pine cone, fir, kite, snake, mole, weasel, deer, crow, mouse, etc.

Dictated sentences

As each new phoneme is introduced, try dictating words and sentences for the group/individual to illustrate. Use a new page for each phoneme.

ar
Mars bar
Park the car
No parking
Farmer Fred
Smarties

Clue words and silly sentences

ACTIVITY 15

Phoneme frames

This is a way to practise spelling in a multi-sensory way.

Magnetic letters (three-dimensional, not letter tiles) help to reinforce letter shape, orientation and sequencing. Only provide letters needed for each individual word to be spelled.

Some children may not 'hear' individual letter sounds/phonemes. If necessary, preliminary work will need to be done to improve auditory discrimination by pushing a counter into each box of the frame for each sound before working with letters.

Resources

- Whiteboard.
- Magnetic letters.

Activity

- Adult draws phoneme frame on whiteboard with box for each phoneme, e.g. cat.

- Child puts letters in correct order and pushes into boxes, sounding out c – a – t.
- Encourage self-checking. This is very important. If the child places letters upside down or in the wrong order ask the child to check for any mistake.
- Adult removes letters from phoneme frame and asks the child to write 'cat'.

Extension: vowel phonemes

- Show the child that two vowels can make one sound, e.g. *oo*, *oa*, etc.
- The child pushes *both* letters into *one* box.
- Use dotted line to separate vowels.

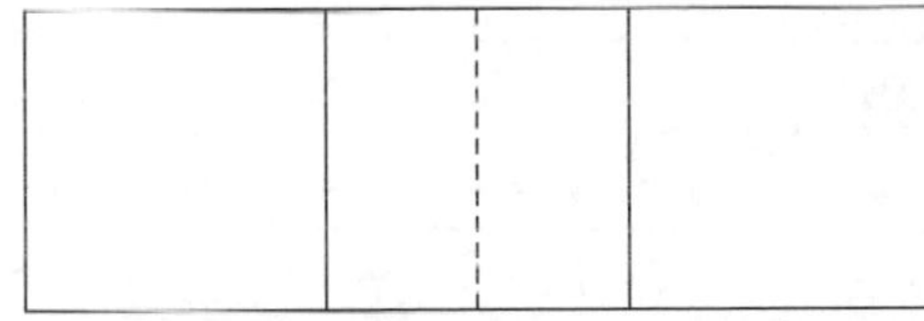

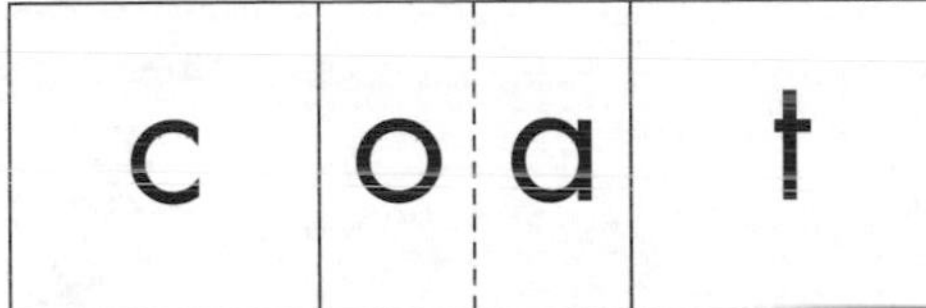

ACTIVITY 16

The alphabet arc 1

This activity is to familiarise children with alphabetical order and letter names. The alphabet forms the basis for acquiring dictionary skills.

a b c d e f g h i j k l m n o p q r s t u v w x y z

It can be used with an individual or a small group.

Resources

- A3-size card for each child, with lower case letters written in alphabetical order in an arc on one side, and a blank arc on the reverse.
- 26 plastic letters (preferably consonants in one colour and vowels in another).

Activity

- Practise reciting the alphabet using letter names.
- With the card facing 'letters side up', adult asks children to place the letters in alphabetical order below the letters on the card.
- Encourage them to start with the *a*, then *z*, then *m*, *n* (my nose) placed centrally, and finally to fill in the remaining letters. (When they are familiar with this, use the reverse of the card without the letter prompts.)
- Practise reciting/singing the alphabet in order. Be careful to articulate individual letters, particularly *l*, *m*, *n*, *o*, *p*.
- Encourage the children to chant the alphabet in quartiles, *a–e*, *f–m*, *n–r*, *s–z*.
- Play games – ask them to close their eyes. Play, *What is wrong?* e.g. Remove one letter, close the gap, open eyes. *Which letter is missing?* Turn a letter upside down. Put two letters out of order. Ask, *how many letters are there? How many vowels are there?*
- Pick out the vowels and place them in order. Check that children can say both vowel sounds and names. Jumble them and ask a child to place them in the correct order. Chant an auditory mnemonic – **a**ngry **e**lephants **i**n **o**range **u**nderpants.
- Ask a player to place the vowels in the correct order on the arc.
- Put three letters into a feely bag for a child to select a target letter by feeling for it.
- Give the child two letters and ask which one comes first in the alphabet.
- Use for memory training – children listen to a series of letters, e.g. ***p s d n***. Children must find the letters and lay them out on the board. Allow them to rehearse 'out loud' if necessary.

ACTIVITY 17

The alphabet arc 2

This activity is to develop phonic spelling skills.

a b c d e f g h i j k l m n o p q r s t u v w x y z

Some children may know alphabetical order but need further practice with the alphabet arc to help develop phonic spelling skills.

It can be used with an individual or a small group.

Resources

- An A3-size piece of card for each child, marked out as an arc.
- 26 plastic letters (preferably with vowels in a different colour).

Activity

- Start by asking the group or individual to place the letters onto the arc in alphabetical order – see Alphabet arc 1 (Activity 16).
- Start with a basic letter pattern, e.g. 'cat', and ask them to make new words by changing the first, then the last letter and finally the medial vowel to make new words. (Adapt according to the skill level that you are teaching.)
- Use the letters to teach concepts, e.g. initial/final/middle sounds.
- Ask them to place the target phoneme below the arc. Say a word for them to make, e.g. *ai*, train.
- Jumble the letters (with warning) and ask children to re-make the word.
- At the end of each session ask them to write down the words that they have made (from dictation).
- Using a pointer, point to a series of letters in order that make a word and ask one player to say then write the word eg. p – l – u – m.
- Use to support the spelling of 'tricky' words – child says the word using letter names, selects the letters and makes the word. Jumble and see if s/he can feel the letters and assemble with eyes closed.
- Play 'Back to the Board'. This game can be used in a variety of ways, e.g. The teacher calls out the word. The group makes it as quickly as possible using the letters. If correct the teacher shouts 'Back to the board' and they replace the letters as quickly as possible to find a winner.
- Use to introduce simple plurals. Child makes the word, adds an 's', then records the word.

ACTIVITY 18

Pattern making

This is a way for children to develop an awareness of patterns in words.

Many children do not instinctively learn by analogy so this must be taught. Poor spellers seem to think that you have to learn every single word anew. They may know a letter string but lack confidence and need encouragement to generate words from it e.g. *–ing* can be used to make *ring, king, sing* etc.

These activities are suitable for individual or small group work.

Resources

- Scissors.
- Card.
- Pen/pencils.
- Paper/whiteboard.

Activity

- Simple games can be played using word cards for spelling patterns, e.g. *and*, *air*, *ump*, *est*, etc.
  - Children sort words into the correct spelling patterns. Start with two families to begin with. Some guidance may be needed to

begin with for the children to identify the spelling patterns. As they become more confident, increase the number of patterns.

- Children each have a card with a different letter string written on it. Adult asks them to write other words with the same letter string on whiteboard.
- Ask children to write as many words with same letter string in one minute (shorter or longer time, depending on ability).
- As a paired activity see who is first to write five or more words correctly using their letter string.
- Play dominoes: match words according to the spelling patterns.
- Play spelling pattern snap and pelmanism.

- Spelling wheels: by spinning the wheel new words are made and recorded. Make the wheels with two circles of card joined with a split pin.

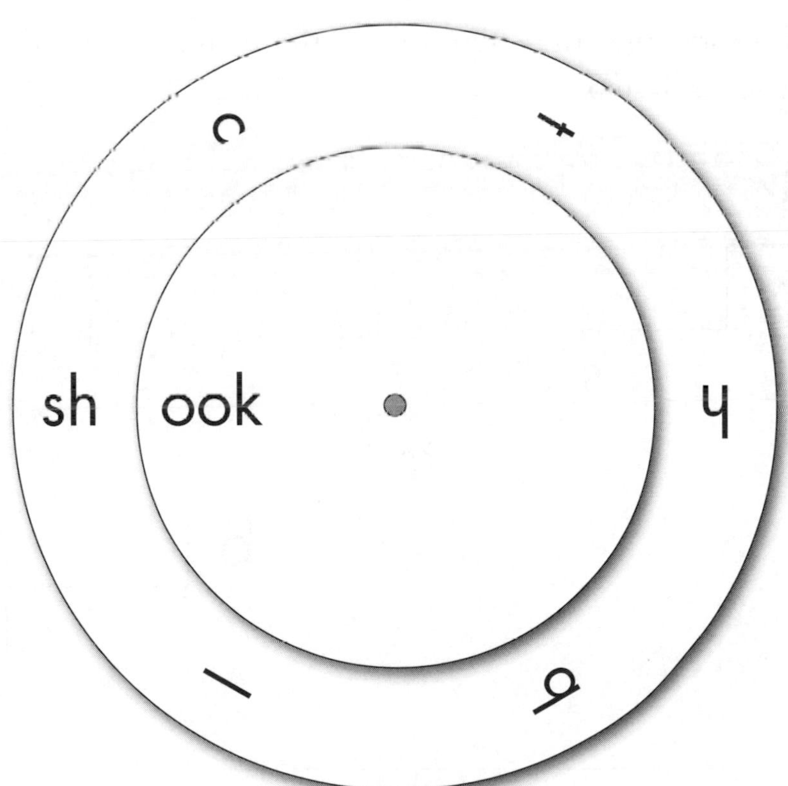

- Spelling ladders: the child follows the pattern by writing a new word on each rung.

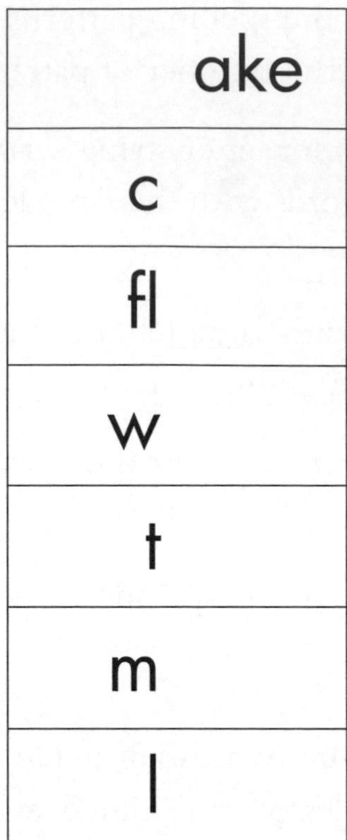

- Spelling staircase: the child follows the pattern by writing a new word on each step.

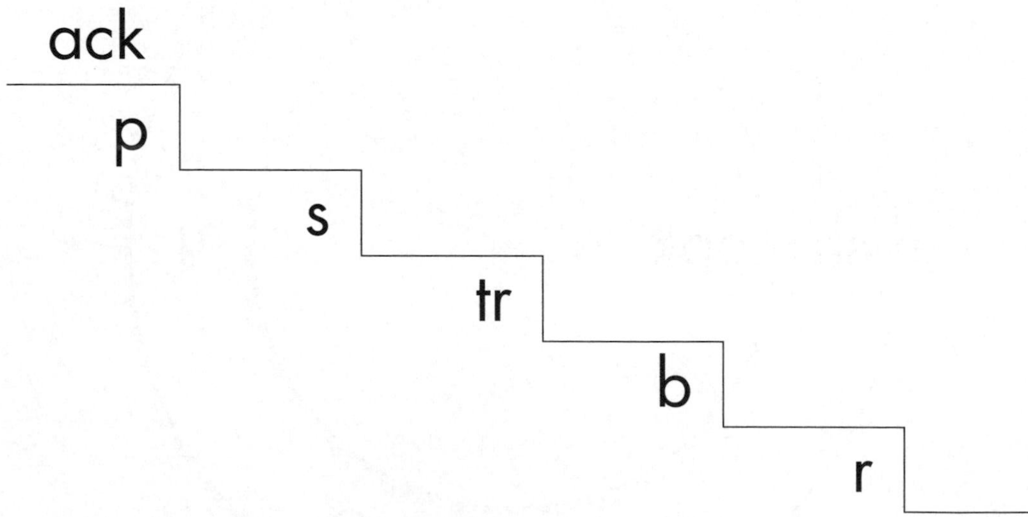

> The resources for these activities are easy to make and allow you to tailor the spelling patterns to an individual child or group. For ready-made resources see for example Smart Kids (www.smartkids.co.uk) and LDA (www.ldalearning.com).

ACTIVITY 19

Spelling stones

This is a way to develop phonic sequencing skills.

Some poor spellers may know individual letter sounds but have difficulty in remembering them in sequence and putting them together to make the complete word. This game uses 'stepping stones' as 'spelling stones' to reinforce phonemic awareness. The child has to concentrate on each letter and sound before jumping on to the next. The act of jumping also provides kinaesthetic reinforcement for putting the sounds in the correct order (and is great fun to do!).

Number of players: one or more.

Resources

- Large sheets of paper or carpet tiles cut roughly to the shape of a stepping stone for each sound.
- For outdoors, chalks and suitable area of playground/path for drawing stones.
- Whiteboards, pens.

Preparation

- Write letters for CVC word on stones.
- Place spelling stones on floor in correct order, or draw three stones

on playground. Explain that the child must step on the stones to 'cross the river'.

Activity

- Child stands by first spelling stone and looks at the three letters.
- Remind child to take care not to fall off into the 'water.'
- Child jumps on to first letter and says sound.
- Child jumps to second letter and then third pronouncing each sound in sequence.
- Child says word.
- Repeat the activity if the child can't say word.
- If child is finding it difficult, the adult can say and blend the sounds as the child jumps.

Extension

- Ask the child to write words used in the activity on whiteboard.
- Score a point for each correct spelling.

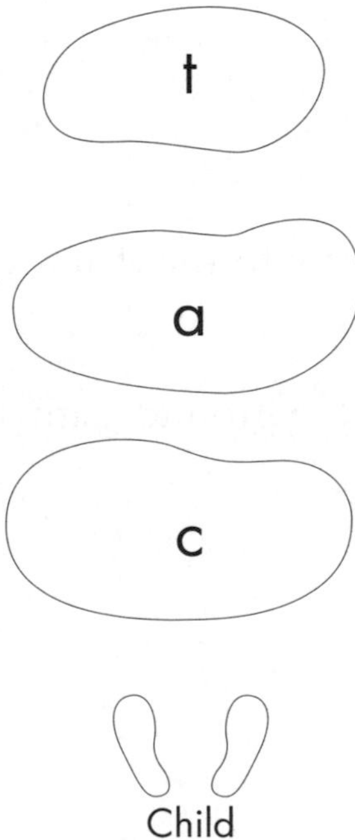

C. Games for spelling practice

Like all the activities in this book, these games are meant to be *fun*. Encourage the child to have a go and to take risks. Start by using a bank of words, which the child can spell, so they are comfortable and successful with the activities. This is so that the child gains confidence before new words are added. Use the games after spelling strategies have been tried out, to see which is the best way for the child to learn and remember spellings.

These games consolidate spellings which the child has already learned. They are designed to provide extra practice and reinforce different spelling skills. They will help children to retain words long-term and achieve automaticity.

All games and activities can have an element of competition in them if required. Some children respond to challenge, others may not; under pressure they make mistakes and lose confidence. It is therefore very important to gauge each individual's response to competition.

- The games have been deliberately kept simple and avoid complicated scoring systems.
- A speed element can also put some children under too much pressure so use this sparingly.
- Fun is essential but accuracy is also most important.

Practise! Practise! Practise!

The activities suggested below are suitable for individual or small group work and might be used as extension activities for many of the games in this section. Many of these activities are ideal for practice at home (some explanation and/or demonstration will be needed). The key is little and often, and five minutes a day is ideal.

- Make a word wall – add two new words at a time. Five ticks on five different occasions and the 'brick' can be coloured in. Re-visit previous words on a regular basis.
- 'Spaghetti' strips – child must write the word five times along the strip.
- 'Buzz' words – write a hollow word or use 'outline' on the word processor. Child must write within the lines without touching the side or teacher makes a buzz sound.
- Write target words onto a bookmark.
- Write target words onto small pieces of card and join with a treasury tag or key ring.
- Have two envelopes labelled *Words I can spell* and *Words I need to learn*. As words are learned they can be added to the appropriate envelope.
- Encourage the child to say the word out loud to a rhythm using letter names f-r-i-e-n-d. Try clapping/hopping as each letter is spoken. This method is useful for pupils with auditory strength.
- Use a Spelling blitz sheet. Write the word in bold at the top of a sheet of A4 paper. Supply a range of writing implements in different colours. Ask the child to write the word as many times as possible using the different pens/pencils and in different colours.
- Make use of a word processor. The child can type out the word as many times as possible in a range of fonts, sizes and colours.
- Use different voices to spell words (letter names), e.g. squeaky mouse, roaring lion.
- Adult writes a word twice, once correctly and then incorrectly. See if the child/group can spot the correct spelling.

ACTIVITY 20

Beat the clock

This is a way to provide extra practice in visual recall.

This game involves being able to picture the word and write it. Using repetition ensures that a word is seen and written more than once in each game. This helps consolidate the target words and develops automaticity.

Number of players: one or more.

Resources

- Clock face or plastic/card clock for each child.
- Whiteboard and pen for each child.
- Twelve strips of card per child.
- Timer for extension activity.

Preparation

Write twelve target spellings on strips of card for each child. These could be twelve different spellings or repetitions (e.g. four words repeated three times).

Activity

- Each child places their cards face down, one on each number of the clock.
- Each child turns over any card, looks carefully at word, then turns card back over and writes spelling on whiteboard.
- Each child turns card over again and checks spelling.
- If correct, card is removed from clock face.
- First to clear whole clock (twelve words) is the winner.

Extension

- Use timer and record time taken to clear the clock.
- Ask the child to try to beat previous time for clearing the clock.

ACTIVITY 21

Clear the board

This is a game for practising individual spelling lists.

It is particularly useful for revising known words to establish automaticity.

It is suitable for two or more players.

Resources

- A base board for each group member as shown.
- A die.
- Six small pieces of card per pupil.
- Paper and pencils.

Preparation

- Each child has a base board and six pieces of card on which are written their individual target words.
- Adult places the cards face up on the board as shown.

said	they	want	when	more	come
1	2	3	4	5	6

Activity

- The pupils take it in turn to roll the die.
- If it lands on '2' the child turns over the card opposite that number.
- Child writes word onto paper/whiteboard.
- The card is then turned over for checking.
- If it is spelled correctly the card is removed from the board, if not it remains word side up.
- The winner is the first one to remove all of the six cards.

Extension

The game can be extended to 12 words if necessary, one board per child. If the die lands on '4' the player can choose to spell either word against the number and so on.

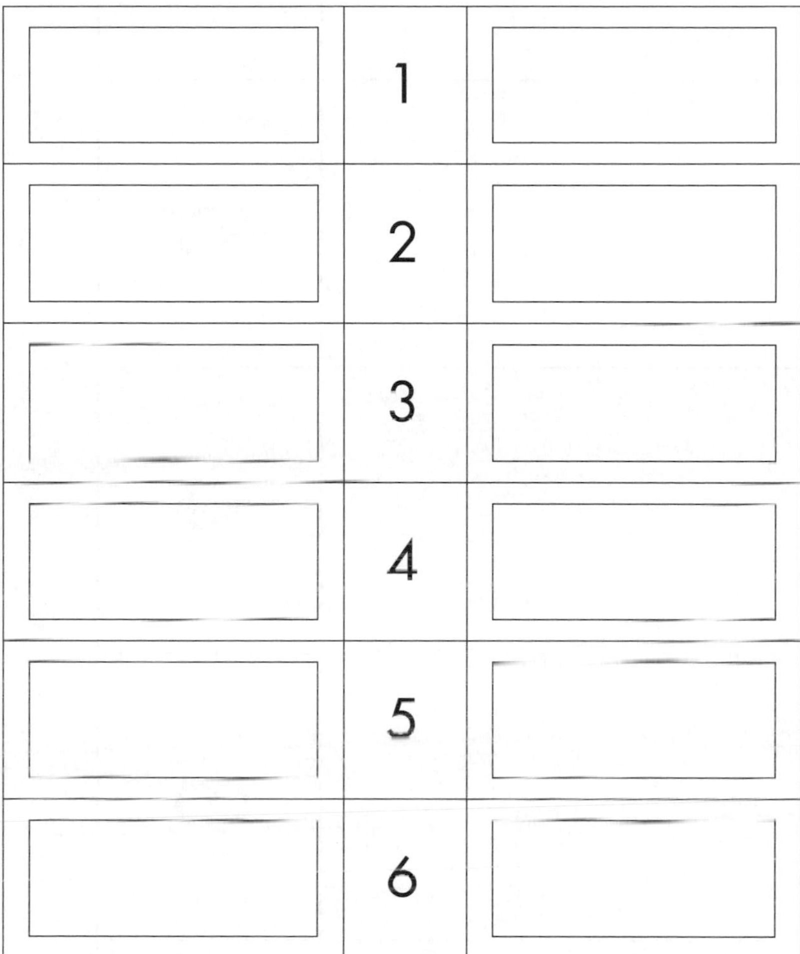

1	2	3	4	5	6

ACTIVITY 22

Dot to dot squares

This is a way to encourage quick recall of known spellings.

This game develops automaticity through encouraging children to look carefully at words and revisualise them. Children enjoy games most where they expect to be successful. This game uses known words so they are unlikely to fail.

Number of players: two or more.

Resources

- Spelling cards from child's bank of known words.
- Dot to dot sheet (page 55) or use large squared paper. A grid of 4×4 dots will make nine squares from 24 successful turns.
- Whiteboard and pen.
- Pencils.

Preparation

Adult selects 15 or 20 spelling cards.

Activity

- One sheet for each game, however many players.
- Child picks one spelling from their own pile.
- Child studies word carefully, turns card over and writes word on whiteboard.
- Child checks spelling by looking carefully at card again.
- If correct child draws one line from one dot to another.
- Next player repeats same process.
- Whoever draws fourth line to complete a square writes their name or initial in that square.
- Continue until all squares have been completed (or first one to reach agreed target number of squares).

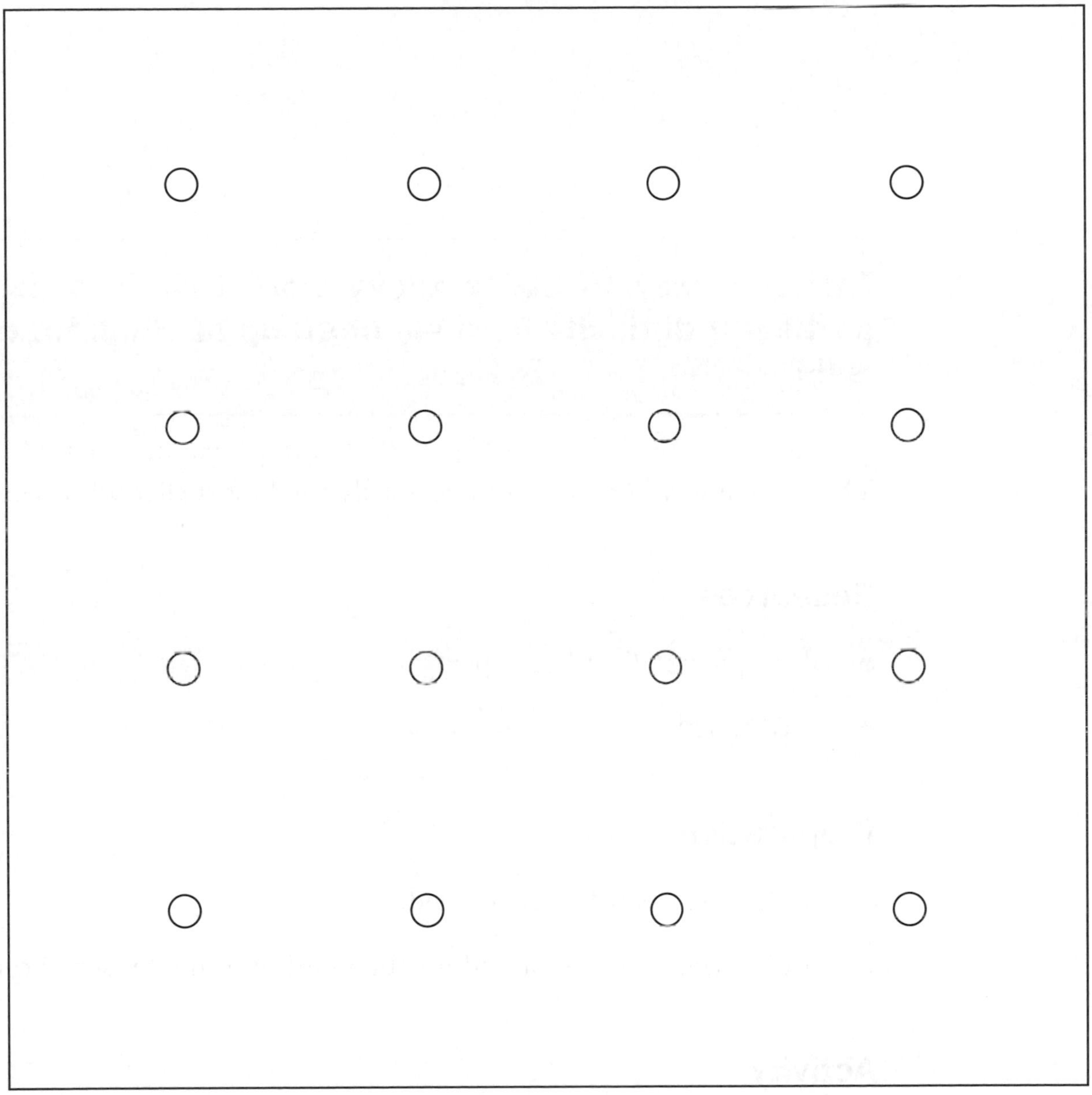

ACTIVITY 23

Follow the leader

This is a way to 'fix' a tricky word that is causing particular difficulty for a small group of children, e.g. 'said'.

This is a game where it is not necessarily the best speller who wins.

Resources

- Blank pieces of card or paper.
- Pens/pencils.

Preparation

- Adult selects word to be learned.
- Adult writes letters required for the word onto master set of cards.

Activity

- Adult makes selected word with master letter cards.
- Children study word and collect appropriate number of blank cards, e.g. *said* needs four cards.
- Children copy letters onto their cards.
- Adult removes master cards.

- Children turn all the cards face down on the table and muddle them.
- Each child in turn picks up a card, aiming to find the first letter in sequence.
- If the correct first letter is turned over this becomes the leader and the child keeps this face up in front of them.
- If the card is not correct, it is turned back over and the next child takes their turn.
- Proceed in the same way with second and subsequent letters.
- The first child to complete the word correctly is the winner.

Extension

This game can also be adapted to practise multi-syllabic words with one syllable being written onto each card.

ACTIVITY 24

Hollow letters

This is a way to encourage quick recall of known spellings.

Some children require extra practice to gain the confidence to use spellings which they have already worked on. This activity encourages quick recall and is a good indicator for the teacher of which words the child can most easily remember. It can be used as a record of a child's progress by showing cumulative improvement in the number of words recalled.

Number of players: one or more.

Resources

- Hollow letter sheet (see pages 59–60).
- Variety of pens, e.g. gel, glitter.

Preparation

- Child chooses or adult selects one letter from the alphabet.
- Adult draws large hollow version of chosen letter (A4-size, or enlarge from the template opposite).

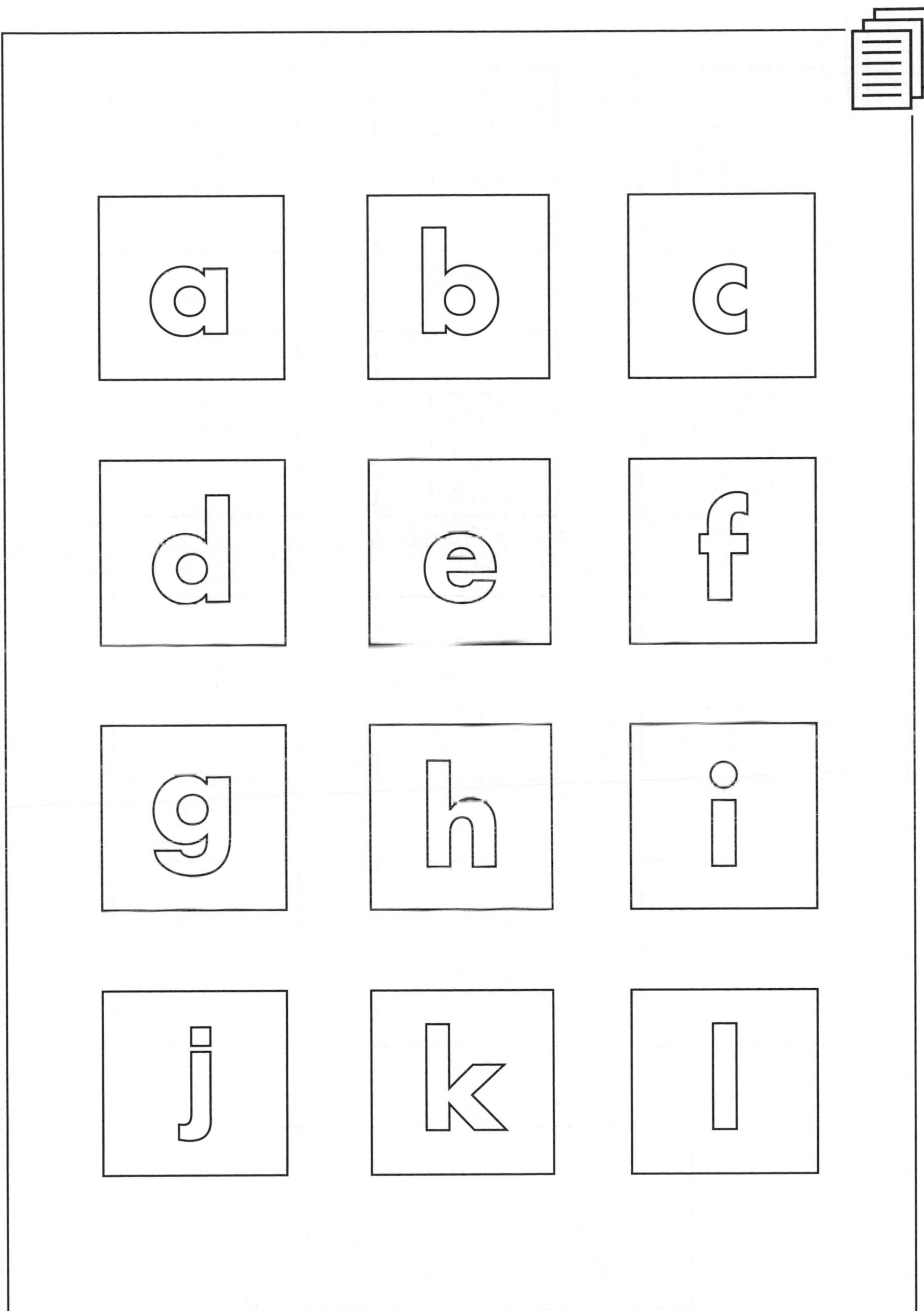
a
b
c
d
e
f
g
h
i
j
k
l

m
n
o
p
q
r
s
t
u
v
w
x
y
z

Activity

- Discuss with the child words they know which begin with that letter.
- Child tries to fill large hollow letter shape with words beginning with that letter.

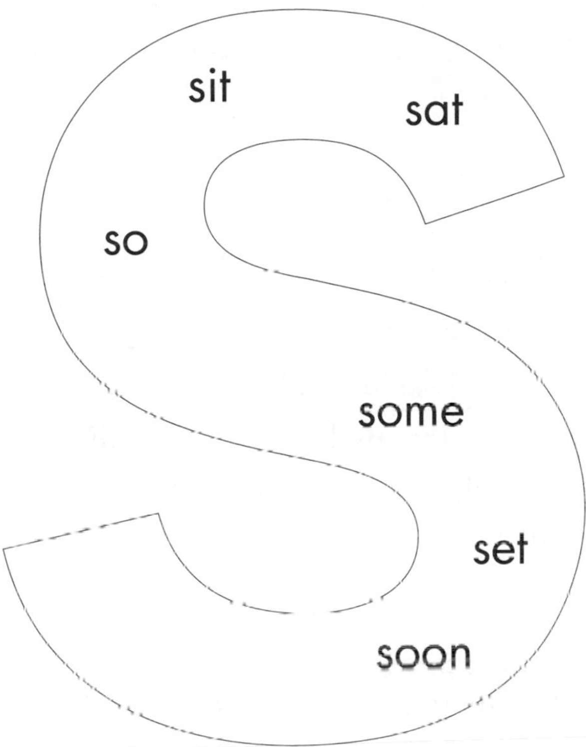

Extension

Write words in a hollow letter which *end* with that letter (only suitable for spellers who are gaining confidence).

ACTIVITY 25

Hopscotch

This is a way to reinforce recognition of spelling patterns.

This is another approach for children who have difficulty in recognising spelling patterns. It helps children to understand that in English the same letter patterns may represent very different sounds. This game encourages them to look carefully at words and visualise common spelling patterns.

Number of players: one or more.

Resources

- Chalks and suitable outside area for writing on.
- Whiteboards, pens.

Preparation

- Draw squares and rectangle on the ground, e.g.

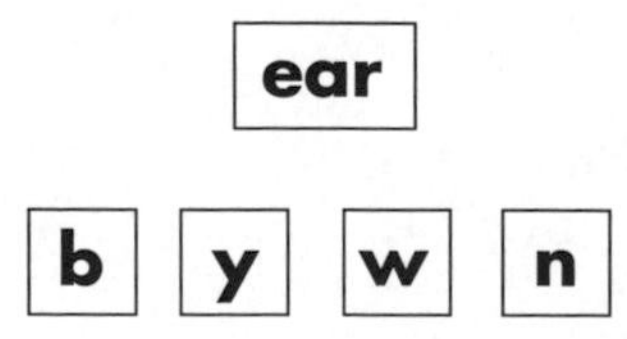

- Write initial letters in squares and spelling pattern in rectangle.

Activity

- Child chooses an initial letter, stands on it and says the sound.
- Child jumps from initial letter square to rectangle containing spelling pattern.
- Child says word.
- Repeat with other sounds.

Once the child is confident with this activity:

- Ask the child to write words used in the activity on whiteboard.
- Score a point for each correct spelling.

Extension

Use the game to teach and practise multi-syllabic words, e.g. re – mem – ber.

ACTIVITY 26

Quick draw

This is another way to practise visual recall of words.

Some children have difficulty in predicting the most likely way in which sounds are represented in words. In this game, they have to revisualise the whole word and the order of letters within it. It helps to build up awareness that all words must have at least one vowel. It is a very good way to practise known, high frequency words.

Number of players: two.

Resources

- Alphabet strip.
- Whiteboards and pens, or paper and pencil.
- Templates of insects/animals/objects with ten or eleven components e.g. beetle/mouse/butterfly/spider/house/car (see page 66).

Preparation

- Each child has a set of cards with known high frequency words.
- Each child chooses insect/animal/object to draw.

Activity

- Children swap their sets of cards
- The first player chooses a word and draws short lines for each letter in the word.

_ _ _ _ _

- The second player guesses a letter, using an alphabet strip if necessary.
- If the guess is correct, the first player writes it in the correct place.
- If the guess is incorrect and the letter is not in the chosen word, the first player can draw or select one portion of the picture (keep a record of letters incorrectly guessed so that the second player does not repeat them – a small whiteboard is good for this).
- The game continues until either the word or picture is complete. A complete word means that the second player has won; a completed picture means that the first player has won.

Extension

- Use longer, more 'tricky' words.
- Use a timer to limit the amount of time allowed to complete the word.

ACTIVITY 27

Race and chase

This is a way to give extra practice in visual recall.

Some children need extra practice to be able to picture words and write them. This game helps visual recall as spelling longer words moves the player more quickly along the racetrack and provides an incentive for tackling long words.

Number of players: two.

Resources

- Race track (page 69) or use a track from any commercial race game.
- Counters or other suitable tokens/toys.
- Card strips (for writing spellings).
- Whiteboard and pen for each child.

Preparation

- Photocopy racetrack (page 69).
- Write target words on cards (different set for each child).
- Keep track short and use fewer words for learners with most difficulties.

Activity

- To start, each player places counter on first square.
- Give each child their partner's set of spellings.
- First player chooses and reads a word aloud (or shows and then hides the word from partner).
- Second player writes the word on whiteboard.
- If correct, second player moves one square along track for each letter in the word.
- If incorrect, player does not move.
- Second player has next turn to 'chase' or race ahead.
- Play continues until one player reaches the finish line.

Extension

Use a longer track, longer words or trickier words.

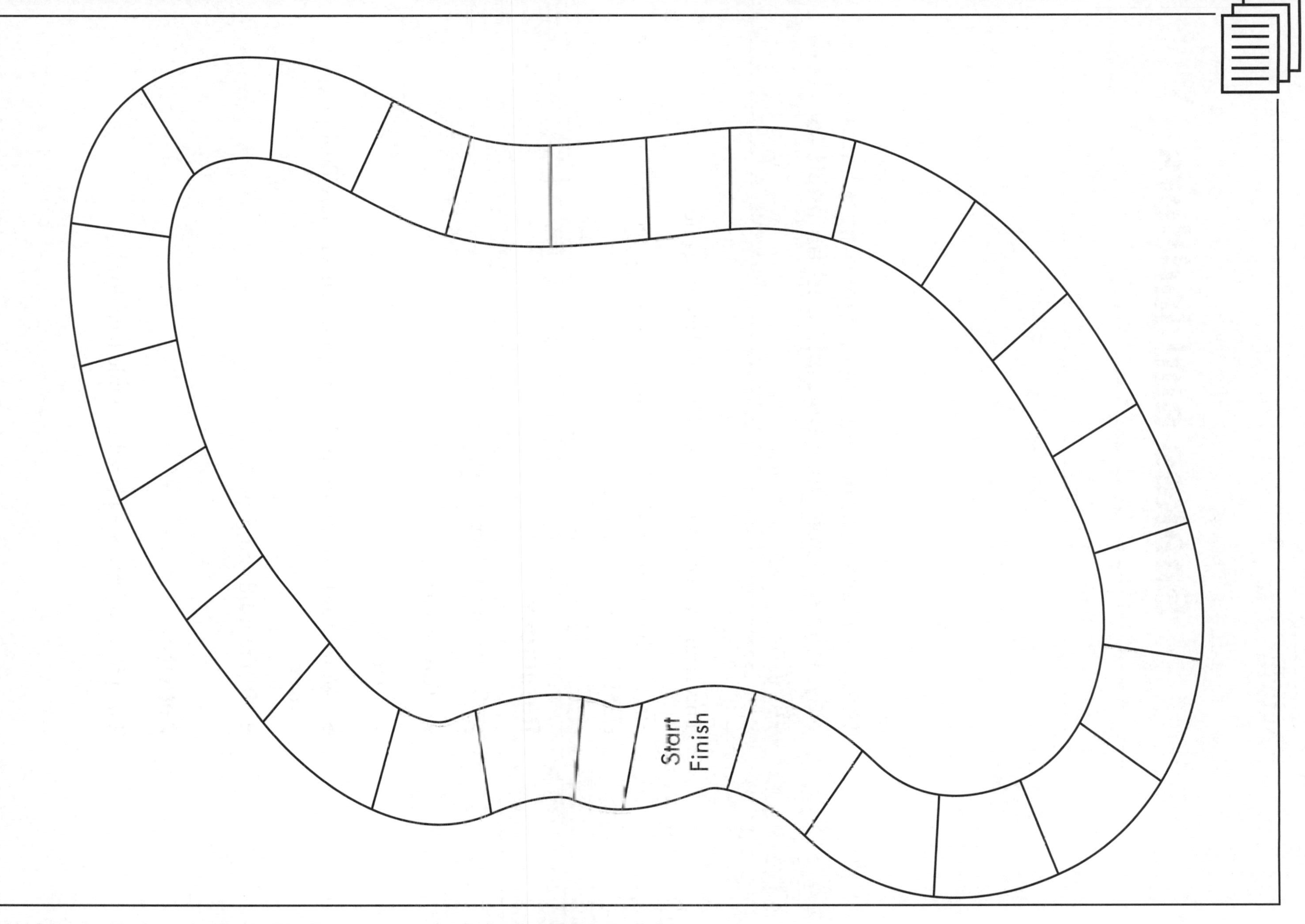
Start
Finish

ACTIVITY 28

Snakes and ladders

This is a method of practising and revising words in a fun way. It is suitable for one child and an adult (or older child).

This is an adaptation of the snakes and ladders game.

Start with five words that have already been learned. Add more as the child develops confidence.

Resources

- Snakes and ladders board.
- Two counters.
- One dice.
- Words for learning to spell written on small individual pieces of card.
- Whiteboard and pens.

Activity

The pieces of card are placed in a pile face down.

Child's turn

- Child throws the dice and moves the number of squares.
- When the child lands on a ladder s/he turns over the top card, reads the word out loud, and places it at the bottom of the pile.
- Child must write the word correctly in order to go up the ladder.
- When the child lands on a snake, s/he turns over the next card, reads it out loud and places it at the bottom of the pile.
- Child writes the word. This word must be written correctly in order to stay there, otherwise s/he must go down.

Adult's turn

- When the adult lands on a ladder the child reads the word then spells it by writing it down. The adult can only go up if the child makes a mistake.
- If the adult lands on a snake s/he must go down if the child spells the word correctly or stay put if the child makes a mistake.

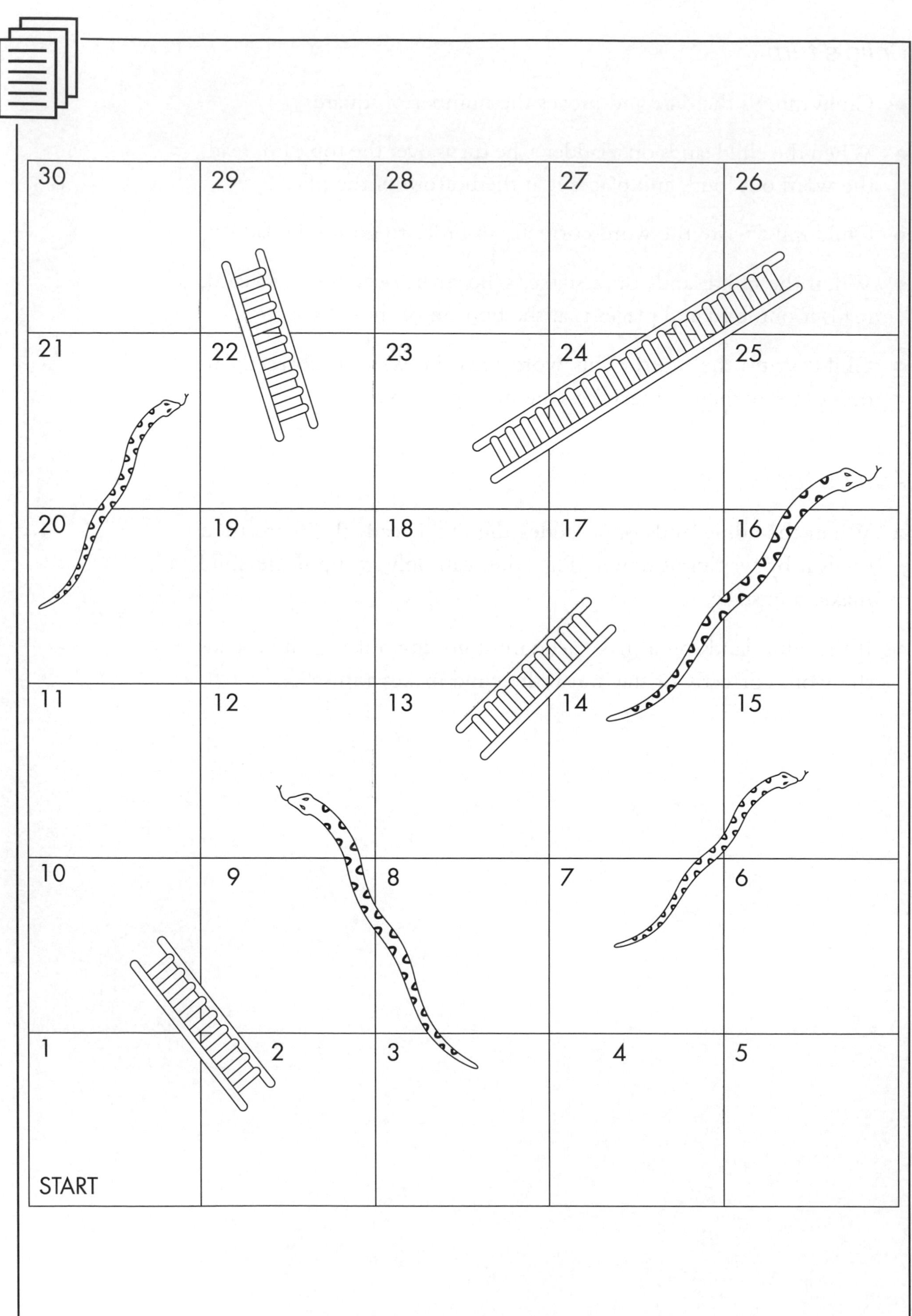
30
29
28
27
26
21
22
23
24
25
20
19
18
17
16
11
12
13
14
15
10
9
8
7
6
1
2
3
4
5
START

ACTIVITY 29

Shannon's game

This is a way to develop awareness of the probable sequence of letters in a word and of common spelling patterns.

Some children have difficulty in predicting the most likely way in which sounds are represented in words. There are probable letter sequences which good spellers readily recall but some children require extra practice to develop this skill.

Number of players: one or more.

Resources

- Alphabet strip.
- Whiteboard and pen or paper and pencil.

Preparation

Adult chooses list of words from bank of words which child can already spell with confidence.

Activity

- Adult writes first letter of word (lower case not capital).
- Adult draws dashes to represent each additional letter in word.

- Child must guess letters in correct sequence, e.g. night

  n _ _ _ _

  n i _ _ _

  n i g _ _

  n i g h _

  n i g h t

- Remind child every word must have at least one vowel.
- Child has up to five guesses for each letter.
- After five incorrect guesses then adult writes in next letter.
- Repeat until word is completed.

ACTIVITY 30

Speed spelling

This is a way to develop automaticity.

Speed spelling is a modified form of precision teaching. The idea is that the child writes the words quickly without having to stop and think.

Speed spelling is not a method of learning to spell words but a way of consolidating the known.

This activity can be used with an individual or small group.

It can easily be done at home.

Resources

- Spelling sheet (page 77).
- Pencils.
- Stopwatch.

Preparation

Adult selects three words for revision, e.g. *said*, *they*, *went*.

Activity

- Adult dictates selected words in random order, e.g. *said*, *said*, *went*, *they*, *they*, *went*, *said*, *said*, *went*.
- Child writes a word in each box.
- Adult times and calls STOP after one minute.
- Adult records the number of words written correctly.
- This should be done daily for a week with the child attempting to beat the previous number of correct spellings per minute.

Name: Date:

Speed spelling!

How many words can you write in a minute?

Number of words correct =

ACTIVITY 31

Spelling pairs

This is a way to promote confidence and support attempts at spelling.

Hesitant spellers who lack confidence benefit from the support of a partner, who can help them by acting as a 'sounding board' for attempted spellings. This encourages the child who is a poor speller to make attempts, knowing that errors can be corrected. Short daily practice (no more than ten minutes) will help reinforce the ability to look closely at words. In particular, it will draw attention to the tricky bits.

Number of players: two.

Resources

- One whiteboard for each pair.
- Pen for each child.

Preparation

Select target spellings from high frequency words.

Activity

- Each pair shares a whiteboard and has a pen each.
- Pairs should sit alongside not opposite each other.
- One is the writer, the other is the helper.
- Adult chooses the spelling, says the word and the writer has a go at writing it.
- The helper checks the spelling, confirms if correct or works with writer to amend until pair agree final spelling for the word.
- After pair agree, adult gives card with correct spelling to the pair and asks them to check.
- Encourage pair to talk about any changes and which was the tricky bit of the word.
- Swap roles between writer and helper before next word.

Extension

This activity can also be used with words from own writing and commonly misspelled words. Ask the child to talk about interesting words such as adjectives or adverbs that they want to use but avoid because they are too difficult. Encourage them to practise these words and use them in free writing.

ACTIVITY 32

Throw the dice

This game is a way to provide extra practice in rapid recall.

It can be played with an individual or a small group. Each child can work on individual spellings. It is ideal for use at home.

Resources

- A die.
- Six small pieces of card per pupil.
- Paper and pencils.

Preparation

- Adult writes a target word onto each piece of card.
- Adult places the cards in a pile word side down.

Activity

- Child picks up the card, reads it then turns it over and follows the instruction for the number thrown.
- Instructions can vary, e.g. Throw a '1' write it once; throw a '2' write it twice etc.

  or

  Throw a '1': write it in red

  Throw a '2': write it three times in green

  Throw a '3': write it with your eyes closed

  Throw a '4': write an enormous one in black

  Throw a '5': say the word aloud using letter names

  Throw a '6': write it six times in blue.
- The instructions can be written onto a large card or a whiteboard.
- If a word is spelled correctly it can be removed from the pile. If not it goes to the bottom of the pile.
- The winner is the one who is first to spell six words correctly.

Extension

If there are still problems with a particular word use the spelling blitz sheet (see Appendix 3).

ACTIVITY 33

Word searches

This is a way to encourage children to look for spelling patterns.

Some children have difficulty in recognising spelling patterns. They need to look more closely at words and spelling patterns within them. Visual discrimination and visual recall can be encouraged by getting the child to search for spelling patterns.

Number of players: one or more.

Resources

- Blank word search grid (page 85).
- Variety of different coloured highlighter pens.

Preparation

- Photocopy one blank grid for each child.
- Prepare word search grid by writing ten target words including vowel phoneme to be learned, e.g. *ee* – tr*ee,* s*ee*d, f*ee*t, etc.
- Write words only left to right horizontally or top to bottom vertically (no reversals or diagonals).
- Fill blank squares with random letters.

Activity

- Adult writes target words at bottom of grid, drawing attention to spelling pattern.
- Child matches and marks words in grid with highlighter pen.

Extension

- Prepare a second grid, without cue words.
- Child finds and highlights target words.
- Child then writes target words on lines below grid.

g	h	s	g	a	f	s	e	e
h	r	t	r	e	e	e	d	p
f	q	r	e	b	k	n	o	c
e	t	e	e	i	f	e	e	t
e	s	e	n	m	o	y	a	b
l	g	t	l	k	z	r	m	x
i	f	s	e	e	d	v	e	c
j	u	c	p	s	h	e	e	p
e	e	l	v	d	w	c	t	b

1 ____________________

2 ____________________

3 ____________________

4 ____________________

5 ____________________

6 ____________________

7 ____________________

8 ____________________

9 ____________________

10 ____________________

1 ____________________

2 ____________________

3 ____________________

4 ____________________

5 ____________________

6 ____________________

7 ____________________

8 ____________________

9 ____________________

10 ____________________

Spelling record sheet 1

Pupil's name: **Adults:**

Word	Date:	Date:	Date:	Date:	Date:

APPENDIX 2

Spelling record sheet 2

Pupil's name: **Adults:**

Word	Start date	Next day	2 days later	Next week	1 month later

APPENDIX 3

Spelling blitz sheet

The word: _ _ _ _ _ _ _ _ _ _ _ _ _ _

Write it three times in black.

Write an enormous one in red.

Write three tiny ones in green.

Write it with your eyes closed.

Write it in capital letters.

Write it in joined letters.

Write it twice in blue.

Write a big one in brown.

Write it in yellow.

Write it four times in pink.

Write a very tiny one in black.

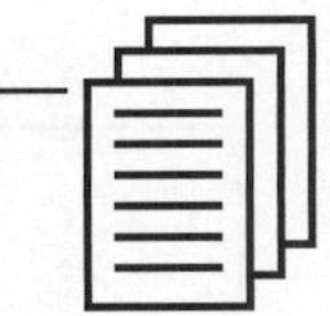

APPENDIX 4

Alphabet strip

a b c d e f g h i j k l m n o p q r s t u v w x y z

A B C D E F G H I J K L M N O P Q R S T U V W X Y Z

APPENDIX 5

Alphabet grid

Aa	Bb	Cc	Dd	Ee
Ff	Gg	Hh	Ii	Jj
Kk	Ll	Mm	Nn	Oo
Pp	Qq	Rr	Ss	Tt
Uu	Vv	Ww	Xx	Yy Zz

APPENDIX 6

Word wall

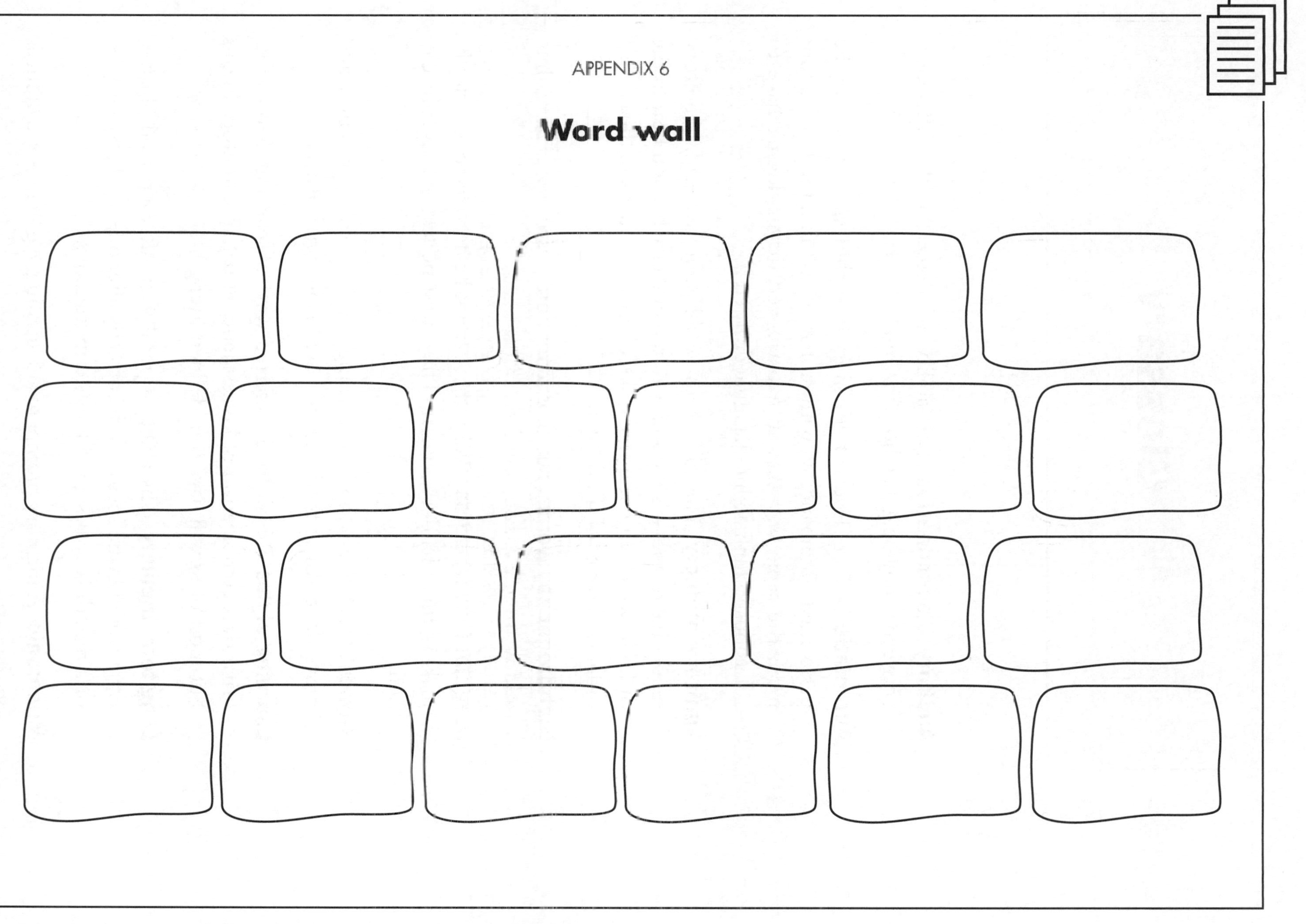

Glossary

Auditory discrimination The ability to detect subtle differences between sounds, e.g. hat/hot, fin/thin.

Automaticity The level of learning is such that a task can be performed 'automatically' without having to think too much about it (in the same way that an experienced driver doesn't have to consciously think about changing gear, etc.).

Auditory memory The ability to recall sounds heard. Auditory sequential memory is the ability to remember what you hear in the order in which you hear it, e.g. a sequence of sounds in the correct order or a series of instructions.

High frequency words The most commonly used words in reading and writing, e.g. said, went, to, from.

Irregular (tricky) words Words that cannot be decoded phonetically, making them harder to learn. They must be learned visually, e.g. said.

Kinaesthetic A method of learning which involves position and movement. Kinaesthetic learners are 'hands on' learners.

Learning styles We all have preferred ways of learning. Most of us learn by a combination of kinaesthetic, visual and auditory means but most of us will have well defined strengths.

Long-term memory The ability to recall facts after a period of time, e.g. the child who spells words correctly after one week, two weeks, or a month later has good long-term memory.

Mnemonic A memory prompt to aid learning, e.g. said = **s**ad **a**nimals **i**n **d**anger.

Multi-sensory The use of as many senses as possible to assist learning – visual, auditory, oral, tactile, kinaesthetic, e.g. 'trace and say' activities such as writing the word in sand engage the learner's senses of sight, touch, hearing and speaking.

Multi-syllabic Words that contain several syllables, e.g. re-mem-ber, sud-den-ly.

Phoneme The smallest unit of sound, e.g. *a*, *ai*, *igh*.

Phonic spelling The ability to write words as they sound.

Precision teaching A technique which enables learners to focus on acquiring a small number of facts, e.g. to recognise a set number of words, numbers or letters within a certain time or to write 10 or 20 known words in a minute. The aim is to achieve automaticity.

Sequencing The ability to retain information (by visual and/or auditory means) and to reproduce it in the correct sequential order, e.g. letters to make a word.

Short-term memory The ability to recall information with immediate response, e.g. the ability to repeat an instruction immediately after it has been given or to be able to repeat a series of letters or numbers.

Spelling pattern Words that contain the same sequence of letters, e.g. and, band, sand, land.

Visual memory The ability to recall a visual image. Visual sequential memory is the ability to remember what you see in the order in which you see it, e.g. the letters in a word, in order to be able to spell it correctly.